Real Racquetball

by Tom Travers and Dr. Tim Miller Ed. D.

Copyright© 2004 by E-force Technologies

Published by EF Composite Technologies L.P.
7920 Arjon Drive Suite A
San Diego, CA 92126
ISBN: 0-9741159-0-8

REAL
RACQUETBALL
TRAINING PROGRAM FOR ALL SKILL LEVELS

ACKNOWLEDGEMENTS

We wish to recognize a number of individuals who gave their professional assistance toward the successful completion of this book:

We are indebted to all the professional racquetball players, including Jason Mannino, Cliff Swain, Sudsy Monchik, Ruben Gonzales, Mike Yellen, Andy Roberts, Woody Clouse, Dan Obremski, Jackie Paraiso Rice, Adam Karp, Tim Doyle and Cheryl Gudinas for sharing their knowledge of the game of racquetball.

We appreciate our typist, Mrs. Laura Carter, for her excellent work. Ted Siller is to be commended for his editing.

We thank Tim Doyle, Cheryl Gudinas and E-Force Racquetball for their commitment to the book. Also, our photographer, Ron Linek is to be commended for his patience and excellence in taking all the photos in this book.

Finally, we are grateful to our families for their support and patience; and most importantly, to God for giving us the ability and desire to complete this book.

IS THIS BOOK FOR YOU?

Are you tired of getting beat time and time again by the same players? Have you been playing racquetball for a long time and feel you're not getting any better? Are you looking to perform at a higher level? Would you like to know the strategies that top professionals use to increase their performance? If your answer is yes to any of these questions, then this is the book for you! This book was created to help players at any level increase their knowledge of the game, improve their game performance, and advance their level of play. In order to achieve these goals, top ranked racquetball professionals were interviewed and have graciously shared their secrets. Their advice, combined with the authors' 40+ years of experience playing, teaching and coaching, makes this one of the first racquetball books ever published to incorporate advanced knowledge on racquetball principles.

CONTENTS

In this book, the following strategies and philosophies will be developed:

INTRODUCTION

I've been teaching and coaching racquetball on the collegiate level for many years. During this time, I've taught numerous beginner and advanced racquetball courses, won a variety of state and local tournaments and coached teams to various state, regional and national championships. I've also been fortunate enough to have coached several professional tour players and many amateur players. I also think that I've read every book written on racquetball and viewed every tape produced that gives instruction on the game. With this background, I thought I knew almost all there was to know about racquetball. However, with the constant rule changes, new developments in racquet size and power and changes to the velocity of racquetballs, I decided to explore the effects these changes are having on the game and its players. In order to improve my game and to assist my players and students in learning new concepts of modern day racquetball, I searched for a top player and mechanics professional. My search led me to a local teaching professional named Tom Travers. Tom's credibility speaks for itself. He has been a head coach of the United States Racquetball Team, a six time national champion at USRA Nationals, and is the author of Mastery of Racquetball, Single and Doubles are just a few of his accomplishments. But it wasn't only Tom's play that impressed me as much as his knowledge of the game. He has studied the mechanics of top professionals and amateur players and has maintained a strong knowledge base on all the new changes in equipment, mechanics and players strategies. Together, Tom and I have teamed to write this book.

Dr. Tim Miller

One of the main reasons I wanted to write this book was to help other racquetball players improve their game and cardiovascular fitness as I first learned from my college physiology professor, Dr. Sander Molnar, at Furman University. Years later I met another professor, Dr. Tim Miller, who sincerely wanted to learn from me everything I knew about racquetball in order to improve his knowledge of the game and to assist the collegiate racquetball team he coaches achieve greater success. With his knowledge on fitness training and coaching combined with my experience and knowledge of racquetball mechanics, we made an excellent team. Tim is a terrific coach and has used his knowledge of racquetball unselfishly to develop numerous young players to the highest levels of excellence. He has coached collegiate players to five national championships. In 2001, the United States Olympic Committee recognized him as Racquetball Developmental Coach of the Year. His desire to learn and practice the principles we'd discussed at great length further encouraged me to team with him to write this book.

I also decided to write this book to share my love for a game that has become a major part of my life. It has improved my quickness, agility and concentration. It has increased my fitness and made me believe in myself. Now it's my goal to share this information in order to help you improve your game and become more confident.

Racquetball has changed dramatically through the years and with these changes, have evolved new strategies and techniques that we will attempt to discuss in this book. It is my hope that you will learn to apply these concepts to your game and see dramatic improvements.

Tom Travers

CHAPTER I

HOW DO YOU PLAY RACQUETBALL?

Racquetball is very easy to learn and play at the beginner level. With one lesson on the basic rules of the game, players often have terrific fun and receive great exercise playing their first match. Many players play for years at the beginner level and use it more for recreational and fitness reasons rather than out of concern for improving. However, for those players who wish to improve performance and advance to higher levels of play, it is imperative that they learn and practice a variety of skills, learn court positioning and strategy, and play, play, play.

In professional play, only one serve is permitted with games played to 11 points in a best of five series. In amateur play, two serves are awarded the server, except in the open division where only one is permitted. Games are played to 15 points, best of three with a tiebreaker to 11 points if needed.

Anyone interested in competing in tournaments has a variety of skill and age divisions, used to equalize the competition, from which to choose. The skill divisions range from lowest to highest amateur divisions including a novice (first year), D, C, B, A and Open (Highest Amateur). There is also a professional tour. The age divisions are broken down as follows: Girls/Boys 6, 8, 10, 12, 14, 16, 18; Men and Women 19, 25,30, 35, 40, 45, 50, 55, 60, 65, 70, 75, 80, 85.

The court dimensions in racquetball are 20' high x 20' wide x 40' long. The service box is located in the center of the court bordered by two parallel lines. The receiving line is located 5' behind the shortline. *(Diagram 1)*

The server can stand anywhere inside the serving zone; both feet must start in the zone. However, when following through on the serve, one foot may go over the front service line as long as part of that foot is touching the line. *(Picture 1)*

The Raquetball Court

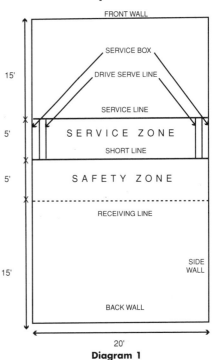

Diagram 1

Picture 1

Picture 2

To receive serve, the receiver stands in the center of the court, about 4' to 6' from the back wall. (approximately an arm and a racquet length away from the back wall) *(Picture 2)*

To start the game, the server must hit the front wall with the ball and the ball must then cross the back service line before hitting the floor. The receiver must return the ball to the front wall, after it crosses the back service line on the bounce, or the 5' line on a fly. Each player then plays out the rally by returning the ball to the front wall. The rally ends when a player lets the ball bounce twice or the ball hits the floor before reaching the front wall. If the server wins the rally, a point is awarded. If the receiver wins the rally, a point is not awarded, however, the receiver wins the serve.

The term "sideout" is used when the server loses the serve. A sideout occurs during the following serves:

1. The ball hits any surface first (side wall, ceiling, or floor) before the front wall.

2. The ball hits the server on a fly.

3. The second serve does not cross the short line or hits the back wall before hitting the floor.

4. The second serve hits two sidewalls after the front wall before bouncing on the floor.

Second serves are permitted in amateur play during the following:

1. The first serve is hit short of the back line of the service box.

2. The first serve hits the front wall then the ceiling.

3. The first serve hits the back wall on a fly.

4. The first serve hits two sidewalls after the front wall before bouncing on the floor.

After serving the ball, the server should move back toward center court near the 5' line keeping an eye on the receiver and preparing for the return. The server should maintain a low center of gravity and be ready to move. The receiver has the option of hitting the ball on a bounce or on the fly.

Picture 3

(Picture 3) However, the receiver may not cross the 5' line unless the ball bounces first. At that point, a player may cross the line and hit the ball. If the ball does not bounce, the receiver must wait until it crosses the 5' line before contact can be made. The players follow through can then cross the line.

Hinders and Screens

The terms hinder and screen is easily confused. A screen occurs when a player cannot see the ball. The ball cannot be seen clearly because your opponent is blocking your view. The receiver may call a screen off of a serve maintaining that the ball is too close to the server's body. However, most screens are called when players are too close to each other where the offensive player cannot see the ball. *(Picture 4)* If a screen is called on a first serve, then a second serve is awarded. If called on the second serve, a sideout is awarded.

Picture 4

There are two types of hinders':

1. Dead-ball hinder

2. Avoidable hinder.

With a dead-ball hinder, an opposing player is usually in the path of a player impeding his movement to get to the ball. If this occurs, the point is replayed. *(Picture 5)*

In the case of an avoidable hinder, a set up shot has been taken away from the offensive player. This may occur when a player is on the ground and cannot get up or a player has been pushed or blocked. In this case, a point or sideout is awarded to the person taking the shot. It is important to remember that an avoidable hinder should be called if a person intentionally or unintentionally gets in the way and prevents an opponent from making a shot. *(Picture 6)* An avoidable hinder is also called when a player hits the ball directly back at himself and

Picture 5

takes a clear shot away from his opponent. Other types of avoidable hinders include loss of equipment which interferes with play and stroke interference. Both of these hinders can be considered dangerous play. It is important to stop all play at that point to avoid possible injury. Screens and hinders can be difficult to call. However, when there is no referee present and you feel you might have been too close to your opponent, a good gesture would be to replay the point.

Picture 6

Timeouts

Each player has the opportunity to call a timeout. In games to 15, each player is awarded three 30 second timeouts. In games to 11, each player has two 30-second timeouts. However, a player taking more than 30-seconds or calling a timeout when they have none left, will result in a technical foul. One point shall be deducted from their score. Each player has two minutes between games and five minutes before the tiebreaker if necessary.

Extra timeouts are allowed for injury and equipment change. Injury includes contact with another player, floor, wall, racquet or ball. This does not include cramping or fatigue. If a player's equipment is considered dangerous to play or the strings break, extra time may be used without penalty to correct the situation.

Technical Fouls

A technical foul is given (one point deducted from the score) for the following infractions:

1. Profanity

2. Excessive arguing

3. Slamming the racquet against the floor or wall

4. Excessive striking of the ball between rallies.

5. Taking over ten seconds to serve or be ready to receive serve

6. Unsportsmanlike behavior

7. Failure to wear approved eyewear

8. Delay of game

9. Threat to the referee or opponent

10. Calling a timeout when none remain

These are just some of the infractions when the referee should give a technical foul. A warning may be given if the referee feels an infraction is not too serious. However, at this point, an explanation should follow to clarify the rules. Many tournament games are played today without the help of a referee, as well as games socially. Each player should step up their sportsmanship and call a fair game between them. It is important to be aware of the rules so you can make a fair judgment in your game.

CHAPTER 2

EQUIPMENT- IT CAN MAKE A DIFFERENCE

RACQUETS

In order to become a better player, get a quality racquet! The basic rule when purchasing a racquetball racquet is that you get what you pay for. Every year, racquetball racquet manufacturers such as E-Force, Ektelon, Head, Pro-Kennex and Wilson, produce a line of racquets that often are new and improved. At least they want us to believe these improvements are significant. This is true on many occasions, but not every time. Although it's not important to buy a new racquet every year, you should always know what's new on the market, improvements that may make your racquet obsolete, whether the new racquet will help you play better or prove to be just a gimmick. The only way to know for sure is to try the new models yourself. Most court clubs have demonstrator models to try, but if this doesn't work, then find someone who has a newer model and will let you try it. Do not purchase a racquet without playing with it for at least one full game. By playing with the racquet for a game, you will become aware of the weight and how the grip feels. A smaller grip is usually more acceptable for most players to use because the racquet can be easily maneuvered in the court. Remember, the single best way to improve your game is to have a racquet with which you feel confident. Also, you should have a minimum of two racquets that are the same make and model and strung at a string tension you prefer. There is nothing more frustrating than playing in an important match, breaking a racquet string on your favorite racquet and being forced to play with a borrowed racquet. By the time you adjust to this unfamiliar racquet, the game will probably be over.

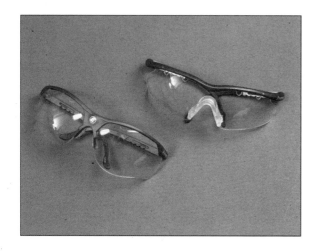

EYEWEAR

WEAR APPROVED EYEWEAR EVERY TIME YOU STEP ON THE COURT!

Eye injury is the number one injury in racquetball. The United States Racquetball Association (USRA) requires all players who compete in sanctioned tournaments to wear eyewear designed specifically for racquetball. These eye guards must be approved by the USRA. Don't learn a lesson the hard way as one of the authors of this book did, by slamming a ball off a wall into his eye and almost detaching the retina. Although it can't be said that eyewear will improve your game, it can cost a match. This could occur when eyewear fits too tight causing excessive fogging, which doesn't allow you to see the ball properly. There are anti-fog treatments that can be applied to the lens of your eyewear that reduce fogging or you may use wet soap and apply it directly to the lens and rinse it off thoroughly. This will prevent moisture build-up. Also make sure your eyewear fits properly and protects your eyes from the side as well as the front.

SHOES

If you are losing matches because of excessive sliding, it may be that the courts are not properly maintained or that your shoes are not appropriate for racquetball. Racquetball shoes need strong side to side support. They need to have a slightly sticky bottom surface that grips the floor enough to keep you from slipping, yet allows you to move with slide steps side to side or run forward or backward quickly. A good quality court shoe made for tennis or basketball should be adequate, however, a shoe designed specifically for racquetball is preferred. Cross trainers and jogging shoes are not always appropriate for racquetball.

BALLS

Racquetballs should have an approved label from the United States Racquetball Association for amateur racquetball play. For important matches, use a new ball, as it's less likely to have lost its resiliency and should play truer. When practicing for an important match, use the same kind of ball designated as the tournament's official ball. For example, don't use a Penn Ultra Blue ball in practice the week before a tournament when in the tournament you will be playing with a Pro Penn Green ball. The slight variation in balls could throw your timing off, costing you some valuable points.

SWEAT BANDS OR HATS

Sweatbands or hats keep the head drier, thus preventing excess moisture from fogging your eyewear. The use of wristbands keep the hands drier allowing you to maintain a better grip on the racquet for better control. Together, headbands or hats and wristbands keep the ball drier (preventing wet ball hinders) and the floor drier (preventing unsafe conditions due to slippery floors).

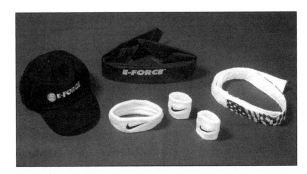

SHOCK ABSORBERS

Shock absorbers are attached to the strings of a racquet generally around the throat area. They are beneficial in acting to reduce the vibration of the ball hitting the racquet and transferring shock waves to the arm and elbow area. Some players insist they absorb shock dramatically, while other players feel the use of these is negligible. For some racquets, they do appear to give some shock absorbing qualities. However, some racquets have shock absorbers already built into the frame.

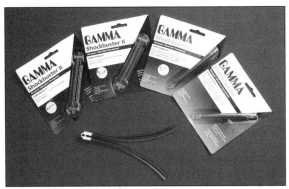

STRING

String tension and gauge are generally related to a players swing speed. Players who swing fast tend to use a lower string gauge (16 – 17ga.). Players who use a higher gauge string (18 – 19ga.) have a more controlled, slower swing. Each person needs to find a tension (26 lbs. – 40 lbs.), which fits their swing speed leading him or her to have the best performance on the court through consistency of shots.

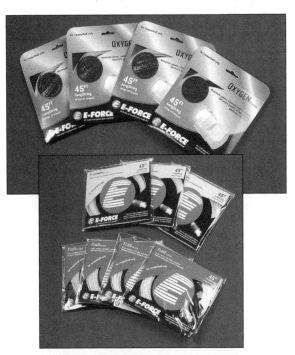

GLOVES

Gloves offer players a better grip on the racquet. It is important to get a glove that feels good on your hand. The glove should breathe properly and have good ventilation for drying quickly. There are different types of gloves available. Some gloves are made for the diving player with more leather on the top part of the last two fingers. Others are made with more ventilation for quicker drying. Whichever the case, be sure to try on the glove so you can determine which one fits the best. It will enable you to grip the racquet better, minimize the racquet slippage and hit the ball harder.

CHAPTER 3

RACQUETBALL MECHANICS FOR THE FOREHAND AND BACKHAND STROKES

It is absolutely essential to learn the correct swing mechanics in order to properly execute the forehand and backhand strokes. Although various instructors and players may vary their technique slightly, the following forehand and backhand techniques are easy to learn and are very effective.

Forehand Grip – The forehand grip is basically a handshake hold on the handle of the racquet as you hold the racquet perpendicular to the sidewall. A V is formed with the thumb as one side of the V and the index finger as the other side of the V. The grip should be firm but not tight or tense, with a slight space between the forefinger and the middle finger. It's basically a common handshake. Advanced players increase power by turning the racquet counter-clockwise in their grip. *(Picture 1)*

Picture 1

Backhand Grip – The backhand grip is formed by gripping the racquetball racquet with a V grip as in the forehand grip but with a slight ¼" turn of the racquet handle toward the floor. When taking the backhand shot, this slight turn helps keep the racquet face perpendicular to the floor at the point of contact with the ball and assists in hitting the ball straight. Advanced players increase power by turning the racquet clockwise in their grip. *(Picture 2)*

Picture 2

Picture 3

Forehand Swing – The forehand swing can be broken down into three stages: the coil, extension and recoil. The forehand stance has your body parallel (especially the feet) to the sidewall. You should watch the ball as you prepare to hit it, keeping your head down, turning your hips a quarter turn toward the back wall, and at the same time bringing the racquet up to the coil position. Then complete the swing as follows:

1. Coil – The wrist is kept straight with the elbow up and the racquet almost parallel to the floor. Hold this position until you are ready to start the actual swing. *(Picture 3)*

2. Extension – The next step in your forehand swing is to step toward the ball with your knees slightly bent. Contact the ball when it's at the heel of the front foot. As you come through the ball, your head, shoulder, arm and wrist form a straight line to the end of the racquet. *(Picture 4)*

3. Recoil – After contacting the ball, the wrist should be snapped to turn the racquet over. Follow the motion through until the racquet reaches the shoulder. A good wrist snap puts speed on the ball. The tip of the racquet precedes the wrist as you recoil (Turn the wrist the same way you would swing a bat or a golf club) proceeded by a good follow through (let your body follow through the swing naturally). As you step toward the ball and swing, use your legs to drive through the ball, keeping the back foot firmly planted while stepping strongly into the ball with the front foot. The hips are turned forcefully toward the ball at the same time giving you maximum power. *(Picture 5)*

Picture 4

Picture 5

Backhand Swing - The three stages of the backhand swing are similar to the forehand swing and include: set position, extension, and follow-through. Remember to grip the racquet as in the forehand grip with a slight quarter turn of the racquet so that the top edge is slightly down towards the floor. This quarter turn helps keep the face of the racquet perpendicular to the floor at the point of contact with the ball. Then complete the swing as follows.

1. Set Position: To get into the set position, move your racquet back into a cocked position as you turn your legs and hips a quarter turn toward the back wall. The wrist stays straight, the elbow is high, and with the upper arm parallel to the floor. The racquet head faces the back wall. Hold the racquet for a fraction of a second. *(Picture 6)*

Picture 6

2. Extension: Step forward toward the ball. Drive the front leg forward, and at the same time drive your shoulder and elbow through the ball. When your elbow is aligned with your front knee, fully extend your arm to contact the ball at the heel of your front foot. Upon contact with the ball, head, shoulder, arm and wrist form a straight line extending to the end of the racquet. *(Picture 7)*

3. Follow-Through: The hips come around as you follow through with the racquet, and your body naturally follows. Hip rotation is the source of power in the backhand as it is in the forehand. With this swing, you can kill the ball from the shoulder height to the ankles. Drive the elbow and shoulder through the ball, extending the arm at the plane of the knee and making contact with the ball. Bend or straighten your front leg to adjust to the height at which you are making contact with the ball. *(Picture 8)*

Picture 7

Picture 8

REMEMBER:
THE GOAL OF BACKHAND AND FOREHAND IS CONSISTENCY AND POWER!!

CHAPTER 4

RACQUETBALL SHOTS AND THEIR MECHANICS

There are a variety of shots used in racquetball that when executed properly prove to be very effective. These shots include: down the line shots, kills, cross court passes, wide angle passes, pinch shots, reverse pinch shots, drop shots, z balls, around the world balls, overhead drives, overhand pinches, ceiling balls, and splat shots. All of these shots are important to have in your arsenal of weapons. In this chapter, we will discuss their proper execution techniques and ideas on when to use these shots. While this chapter will emphasize proper mechanics and how to execute certain shots, the next chapter (5) will thoroughly discuss when to use these same shots strategically to score more points and win matches.

Down the Line – The down line shot should hit the front wall approximately 18" – 20" high. The ball then travels straight back close to the wall, inside the service line. Keep this shot off the sidewall, unless it hits very deep in the backcourt. The ball should hit the floor twice before hitting the back wall. Maintain your consistent swing and follow-through. Remember to execute this shot with good forehand mechanics. *(Picture 1 and diagram 1)*

Picture 1

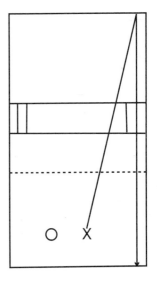

Diagram 1

Kill Shot – The kill shot can be hit from any area on the court. The ball contacts the front wall 1" – 2" high and is hit so low it ends the rally. You should use proper forehand mechanics (or backhand mechanics if hit to the backhand side) making sure your feet are set and you can take a full swing. Remember the coil, extension, and recoil. Don't try to execute a kill shot when you are off balance or when the point of contact with the ball is high. *(Picture 2 and diagram 2 & 3)*

Picture 2

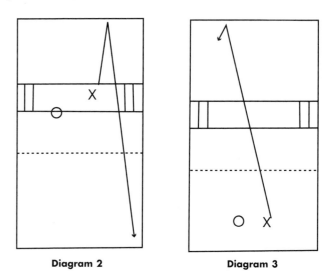

Diagram 2   Diagram 3

Cross Court V Angle Pass Shot – The ball is hit with proper forehand or backhand mechanics (depending on the side you hit the ball on) contacting the front wall 18" – 20" off the floor and traveling in a V angle to the opposite corner. To execute the cross court V pass, your front foot should open at an angle pointing toward the direction you are aiming the shot. It's important to step into the ball and strive to keep the ball from hitting the sidewall. The ball should bounce twice before it hits the back wall. *(Picture 3 and diagram 4)*

Picture 3

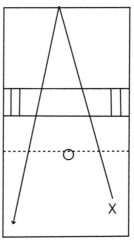

Diagram 4

Cross Court Wide Angle Pass Shot – The cross court wide angle pass shot contacts the front wall slightly left of center that creates a wider angle that sends the ball into the side wall and then into the center court. Pull your front foot slightly over to the right, to the point in the direction that the ball will travel to the front wall. Maintain a consistent swing and follow through. The wide angle is used more in the game today because it forces your opponent to move in several directions to retrieve the shot. *(Picture 4 and diagram 5)*

Picture 4

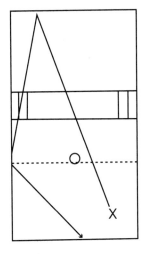

Diagram 5

Pinch Shot – The pinch shot is hit by taking your normal forehand or backhand swing (depending on the side of the wall your hitting the ball) hitting the ball 1' – 2' high and 2' – 3' feet from the front corner, then travels toward the center of the front wall 2" – 3" high to end the rally. Step into the ball as you execute the shot and maintain a consistent swing and follow through. *(Picture 5 and diagram 6)*

Picture 5

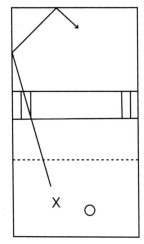

Diagram 6

Picture 6

Reverse Pinch Shot – The reverse pinch shot is hit to the sidewall opposite your racquet hand. For a right-hander, the ball hits the left side wall first, about 1' – 2' high and 2' –3' from the front corner, then travels toward the center of the front wall 2" – 3" high to end the rally. Point your front foot in the direction the ball is to travel, and step into the ball. Maintain your consistent swing and follow-through. *(Picture 6 and diagram 7)*

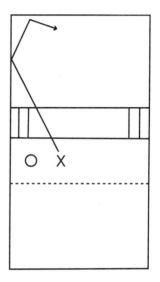

Diagram 7

Drop Shot – The drop shot is hit using a slow, gentle swing dropping the ball into the corner, hitting either the sidewall or front wall first, no higher than 6". Always follow through even though this is a soft finesse shot. *(Picture 7 and diagram 8)*

Picture 7

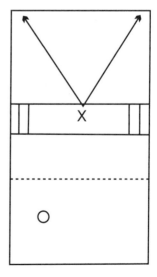

Diagram 8

Z-Ball – The Z ball is hit anywhere from your head to your knee height and can be hit to either the left or right side of the court. Hit the Z shot so that it first contacts the front wall close to the corner. Step toward the corner you're hitting to, and follow through with your swing. The Z should be hit high on the front wall in order to force the ball to come diagonally across court to hit deep on the opposite side wall and run parallel along the back wall, creating a difficult return for your opponent. *(Picture 8 and diagram 9)*

Picture 8

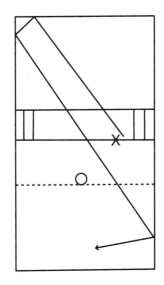

Diagram 9

Around the World Ball – The around the world ball can be hit from above your head to knee high. Hit the shot high on the side wall, about 3' from the front corner. The ball hits high off the front wall, hits the opposite side wall, then should hit deep court and drop close to the back wall. *(Picture 9 and diagram 10)*

Picture 9

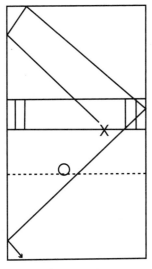

Diagram 10

Picture 10

Overhead Drive – The overhead drive is taken in deep backcourt when you have to hit the ball high and over your shoulder aiming the ball at the front wall 18" – 20" high. With your body parallel to the sidewall, rotate your hips as you reach up and extend, step forward and hit with the motion of the overhand baseball throw. Be sure to follow through on the downward stroke. *(Picture 10 and diagram 11)*

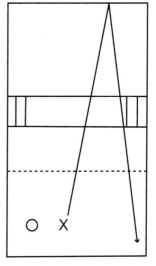

Diagram 11

Overhead Pinch – The overhand pinch can be hit from anywhere on the court. To hit the shot, contact with the ball should be made above the shoulder. The ball hits the sidewall 6" off the floor then the front wall 2" – 3" high. The mechanics are the same as the overhead drive except the ball is aimed toward the sidewall, hitting a few feet from the corner. With your body parallel to the sidewall, rotate your hips as you reach up and extend, step forward, and follow through on the downward swing. *(Picture 11 and diagram 12)*

Picture 11

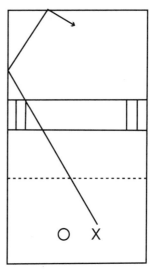

Diagram 12

Ceiling Ball – The shot is hit to the ceiling (or it can hit the front wall first provided the ball next hits the ceiling) within 1' – 2' of the front wall, and travels straight back as close to the side wall as possible without touching the side wall. The ball should hit the floor twice before it hits the back wall. Don't let the ball come off the back wall as a set up. A good rule for hitting ceiling balls on most courts is to aim for the front lights on the ceiling, giving the ball the right angle off the ceiling and into the back court. *(Picture 12 and diagram 13)*

Picture 12

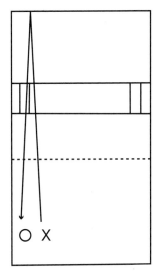

Diagram 13

Splat Shot – The splat shot is hit with your normal swing mechanics hitting the ball very hard and very low into the sidewall with enough power that is compresses the ball. This force kicks the ball farther into the front wall. Point the front foot in the direction the ball is to travel, stepping into the ball and following through. *(Picture 13 and diagram 14)*

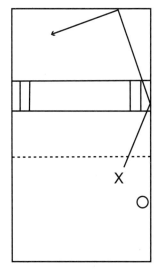

Diagram 14

Picture 13

CHAPTER 5

STRATEGIC SHOT SELECTION

The strategic part of the game is the most critical in learning how to win. After all, in the end, your win/loss record depends on your overall shot selection. It is important to know when to use most shots and why, but it can also be helpful to have an idea of your opponent's game to make better use of those shots. Remember, for a general strategy, high percentage shots are passes from the back third of the court. Kills and pinch shots should be more frequently hit from the front third of the court. The player who makes the least number of unforced errors will usually win the match.

Let's review several shots and when it's appropriate to use them:

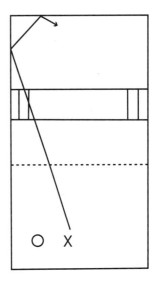

1. **Pinch Shots** – The pinch shot is one of the best scoring shots in racquetball. To reach advanced levels of play, you must execute a good pinch shot. Pinch shots are most effective when your opponent is caught behind you in deep backcourt or behind the service line. It's also effective when your opponent is stuck against the sidewall beside you. Pinch shots should always hit a sidewall first then the front wall at a sharp angle away from your opponent. These shots should be as low as possible without skipping. In order to hit effective pinch shots, your feet should be turned toward the sidewall you are targeting, at a slight angle perpendicular with the back corner. It is important to take a full swing with good forehand or backhand mechanics (depending on which wall your feet are facing) making sure you don't push the ball. Pinch shots may be taken from deep back court (especially if the ball comes off the back wall as a setup) if your opponent is staying in the back court too far, but are usually not as effective when your opponent has time to obtain a center court position.

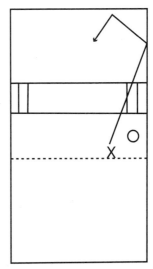

Pinch Shots

If you remember one general rule to effective court management it is this – pinch or kill straight in when you're in the front court and your opponent is stuck in the back court. Take a pass shot when you're in the backcourt and your opponent is in the front court.

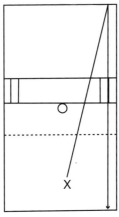

Down The Line

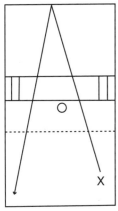

V Pass

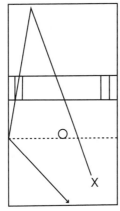

Wide Angle

Pass Shots

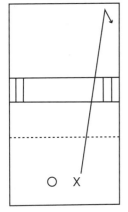

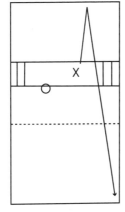

Kill Shots

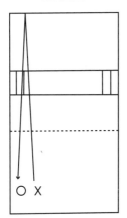

Ceiling Shots

2. **Pass Shots** – There are three types of pass shots: a straight shot down the line, a V shot and a wide-angle pass. The down the line pass shot is most widely used with your opponent pinned to one side or in the front of the court. A V pass is used when your opponent is up front and toward the center of the court. The wide-angle pass is used more in today's racquetball than ever before. The wide angle makes your opponent move in several different directions before getting to the ball. The ball should hit the front wall, then the side wall (close to the service box), then kick down at an angle toward the back wall. When your opponent is against the wall, he/she can be in front or back court when the V pass is used. The direction of both types of V shots is aimed towards each opposing corner to be most effective. Remember, the goal of the V pass is that the ball should bounce twice before coming off the back wall. On the left are examples of the V pass.

3. **Kill Shot** – The third type of shot is the basic kill shot. The kill shot can be used almost anytime. It is most effective when your opponent is in deep court. It is hit as low as possible off the front wall, not allowing your opponent enough time to hit it before it bounces twice off the floor. Remember, when hitting the kill shot, it is important to take a full swing through the ball with a proper follow-through. When taking this shot, be sure to angle it away from your opponent. The kill shot is very popular as it is an offensive shot that scores many points and should be tried at every opportunity.

4. **Ceiling Shots** – The ceiling shot is used primarily as a defensive shot that moves your opponent out of the center court into the backcourt, which will allow you to have time to get in position to take a better shot. Ceiling shots can also be used when you are off balance and not sure exactly what shot to take giving you more time to position yourself for a better shot. To hit the ceiling shot, hit the ball to the ceiling, first aiming approximately 1' – 2' from the front wall. The ball should then hit the front wall and go to the floor, bounce once on the floor, landing near the back wall. When the ball does hit the sidewall or back wall before hitting the floor twice, it is generally an easy set-up for your opponent and should be avoided at all costs. Remember, the purpose of the ceiling shot is not to score points, although if done properly, you may occasionally score.

5. **Around The World Shot** – The around the world ball is hit hard, high and in a direction that enables it to hit four walls. It is a shot that is primarily used to change the pace of a game by forcing your opponent into the deep backcourt. This shot should be used sparingly and primarily as a defensive shot, as hitting it too frequently allows your opponent to anticipate it and cut it off in the air up front as an offensive kill shot.

6. **Z-Ball Shot** – The Z-ball is used to drive your opponent toward the backcourt. To hit the Z-ball, hit the ball into a front wall corner at an angle that hits the front wall first, then carries off the side wall and travels to the backcourt. The Z-ball is used primarily when your opponent is in front or beside you on the court. It should be used to produce a shot your opponent is not expecting that successfully changes the pace of the game.

7. **Fly-Kill** – The fly-kill is a kill shot that is hit in the air before the ball hits the floor and is low enough or at such an angle that your opponent is unable to return it. The fly kill should be taken when your opponent is trapped to the side of you or behind you and does not have enough time to react to the ball.

8. **Drop Shots** – The drop shot is hit from any height or any position on the court. Using a slow, gentle swing, drop the ball in the corner, hitting the sidewall or front-wall first, no higher than 6". This is a very soft shot that is especially effective when you are in the frontcourt and your opponent is in back court or you're both side by side in the backcourt.

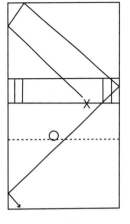

Around The World Shot

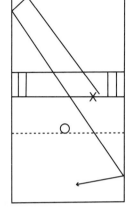

Z-Ball Shot

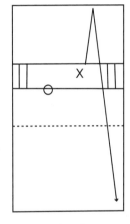

Fly-Kill

In summary, shots need to be taken to maintain center court position. Once a player has control of center court (at the 5' line) or has the opponent in a defensive position (on the wall or out of position – forward or deep backcourt), an offensive shot can be taken to end the rally. Good strategic shots dictate the flow of the game. When you are in front of your opponent, kill the ball. (Pinch, reverse pinch, straight in or crosscourt) This is the zone a player has the highest percentage to kill the ball. When you are behind your opponent, you should pass the ball to the backcourt to make your opponent move. (V pass, straight pass, wide angle) The idea is to work your opponent with shots that put you in the best offensive position to kill the ball.

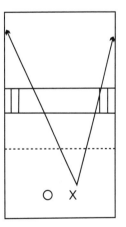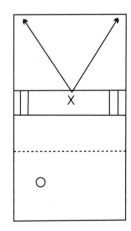

Drop Shots

CHAPTER 6

SERVE PHILOSOPHY AND SERVE MECHANICS

The professionals we surveyed all agreed that the goal in serving is to hit a serve that will force the weakest return possible from your opponent. Cliff Swain, Tim Doyle, Cheryl Gudinas, Jackie Paraiso-Rice, Andy Roberts, Mike Yellen and Dan Obremski all suggest changing your serve frequently; mixing several different serves keeps your opponent off balance, thus forcing weak returns.

Professional Tour Champion, Sudsy Monchik exclaims, "You are in control of the rally from the start! So, score a point now!" Racquetball professional Woody Clouse says, "Go for an ace or put your opponent into a defensive position." Cliff Swain, many years the top ranked player on the pro tour tells us to "play a smart serve and go for a player's weakness". Andy Roberts, who recommends changing the speed of your serves frequently, made a good suggestion. Women's Professional Tour Champion, Cheryl Gudinas, says "Changing your serve for each opponent is a must, however, use serves that you have high percentages of hitting." Cheryl also says, "Base your serving strategy on your strengths first and your opponent's weakness second." In other words, if the right serve against your opponent is a drive serve to the forehand, but you can't hit a consistent drive to that side, chip away until you find something that attacks that weakness, but also allows you to stay within yourself. If you find something that is working, stick with it until that opponent proves he can handle it.

Tim Doyle says, "Put the ball in play with powerful drive serves angling away from the opponent and into the corners of the backcourt." This puts extreme pressure on opponents to react and choose the best return in a matter of a split second. If the opponent does not choose correctly or execute the shot, you will be able to have a variety of shots to end the rally.

We believe that in the amateur levels where players are permitted two serves, that on the first serve you should most frequently go for an ace serve (a serve that can not be returned). This serve should be the serve you have the most confidence in and one that cannot be returned. It is often a drive serve that cracks out. This is accomplished by drive serving to the opponent's forehand or backhand keeping the ball low, at a sharp angle towards the back wall, trying to make the ball bounce twice before it hits the back wall. It is our belief that it is better to be short with this serve than to hit it too high and allow the ball to come off the back wall as a setup. The drive serve should be rotated between the forehand and backhand frequently in order to keep your opponent off balance. Also, you should mix these serves up every so often with another type of serve, such as a jam serve or a Z serve, in order to further confuse your opponent and prevent them from anticipating your serves. When you serve the second serve, generally hit a defensive serve that does not set the receiver up to kill the ball. This is best accomplished with lob serves such as high lobs, half lobs, and Z lobs. It should be the serve with which you feel the most comfortable and which you do not skip the ball, because if you blow this serve you lose the serve. Also, you do not want to place your opponent in a position to win the point.

When you only have one serve, as in most open division tournaments and the professional ranks, your strategy may change slightly. If you cannot consistently make great drive serves that either crack out or stay off the sidewalls or back walls as set-ups, then you should use the second serve strategy mentioned above. However, if you can hit these serves consistently, then stick with them, go for those aces, and take a chance on making a few short balls.

Always remember these serve strategies are ideas that we feel should be used in the majority of situations and cannot be used every time against all players. You must adjust to your opponent. Some players cannot hit lob serves as they are very impatient and want to kill every shot. If you are patient, they probably will give you plenty of shots to kill for points. Opposite of these impatient opponents are those players who want to slow everything down to a snail's pace. With these type of players, you may wish to drive serve on every serve, quick serve, and generally use strategies that speed the game up. Also a good strategy to use in early parts of the game is to experiment with different types of serves and make mental notes as to which serves cause them the most problems. Then, use these serves often or go to these serves in critical situations. Remember no matter which serve strategy you may use, the major goal of serving is to force your opponent into situations, whereby they hit weak returns.

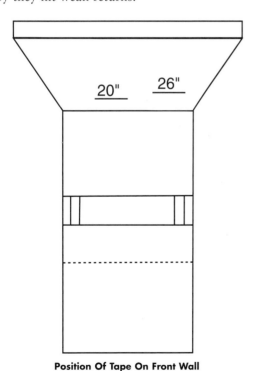

Position Of Tape On Front Wall

The Serve – The serve is the only time that you have complete control of what you do in a game; you have all the time you need to set up for the shot, and to execute the exact power and placement that you want. It's a golden opportunity. Don't rush. Don't waste the advantage. Your objective in serving is to keep the ball away from your opponent's power, and make your opponent take a poor shot. Following your serve, you must move back close to the five-foot line, toward the center of the court to put pressure on your opponent.

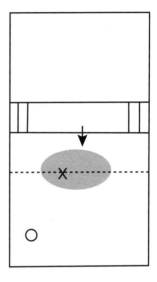

Center Court Position

Developing Service Accuracy – For practicing drive serves to the forehand and backhand, place two strips of easy-to-remove dark tape on the front wall, one on the left-hand side (a racquet-length high) as a target for the serve to the backhand, one on the right-hand side (about 6" higher than the other tape) as a target for the serve to the forehand.

The practice markers help you focus mentally on a front wall zone as you concentrate on your serve. Look at the tape before you serve and visualize the mark on the wall. Then, concentrate on the ball, and on hitting the front wall slightly below the tape. Keep your head down, watch the racquet strike the ball, and follow through.

THE TWO-STEP APPROACH

The two-step approach builds momentum as you step forward into the service motion. Begin in the center court area of the Service Zone, and use the entire area between the Short Line and the Front Service Line as you serve.

Facing the sidewall, put your left foot in front of your right foot along the short line. To avoid a foot fault, no part of either foot can extend over the shot line during the service motion. *(Picture 1)*

Step One: With your right foot, take a step back and a little forward as you drop the ball. The ball and your right foot touch the floor at the same time. *(Picture 2)*

Step Two: Step forward with the left foot, swing and follow through. *(Picture 3)*

Picture 1

Picture 2

Picture 3

Picture 4

Picture 5

THE SERVES

Drive Serve to Forehand

The drive serve to the forehand is executed by dropping the ball slightly back and toward you. Hit the ball farther back (from the heel of the front foot) and closer to your body than you hit a drive serve to your opponents' backhand. Keep your footwork and swing the same as for a drive serve to the backhand. Hit the ball about 26" high on the front wall and angle the ball to the back corner. It's the V angle that makes this serve successful. Do not hit the ball straight back for an easy forehand return by your opponent. *(Picture 4 and diagram 1)*

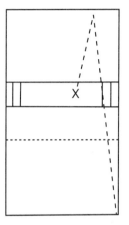

Diagram 1

Drive Serve to Backhand

Stand a foot or so right of center court. Make contact at the heel of your front foot and hit the ball 18" – 20" high, and at an angle so the ball goes to the opposite back corner. Keep the ball close to the sidewall and away from your opponent. *(Picture 5 and diagram 2)*

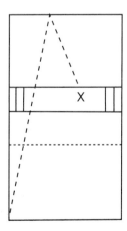

Diagram 2

Jam Serve

This serve is used to keep your opponent from turning their feet. Stand toward the center of the service zone. (A foot or so right of center court) Hit the drive serve 18" – 20" high left of center court so the ball angles toward the side wall and then directly into the receiver, bouncing at their feet. *(Picture 5 and diagram 3)*

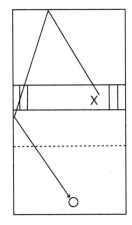

Diagram 3

Picture 5

Drive Z Serve

The opposite corner becomes your front wall. The corner is your target and that is the direction of your footwork. Hit the ball 2' – 3' high on the front wall about 1' from the corner, the ball hits the side wall, bounces as it goes deep to the opposite sidewall, and pops out parallel to the back wall. The drive Z serve forces your opponent into the backcourt. *(Picture 6 and diagram 4)*

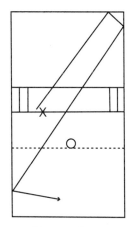

Diagram 4

Picture 6

3/4 Drive Z Serve

The 3/4 drive Z is hit higher on the front wall and 1' from the corner so that your opponent has to return a ball that is chest height in the deep court. It is harder for your opponent to put power into a return at chest height.

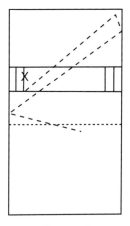

Picture 7

Short Drive Z Serve

A more difficult, but effective Z serve, the short drive Z cuts very close to the short line, hits the side wall and pops out. It is executed the same as a regular drive Z, except that the ball hits the front wall within 6" of the corner. The short drive Z can surprise an opponent who is expecting a deep court serve. To execute, step with back foot first, watch the racquet hit the ball and follow through. *(Picture 7 and diagram 5)*

Diagram 5

Straight Lob Serve

Standing close to the sidewall in the service zone, the straight lob is hit high on the front wall, 3' from the ceiling. The ball comes straight back and close to the sidewall without touching. The ball should bounce twice before hitting the back wall. When serving, hit the ball gently with a lifting motion, as the ball is on its way up from the service bounce on the floor. With all lob serves (straight, angle, nick) it is important to keep your wrist stiff as you make contact with the ball. *(Picture 8 and diagram 6)*

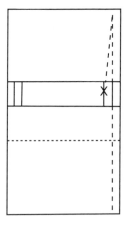

Picture 8

Diagram 6

Angle Lob Serve

From the center of the service zone, the ball hits high on the front wall, 3' from the ceiling, then bounces at the receiving line and then bounces a second time deep into the backhand court. *(Picture 9 and diagram 7)*

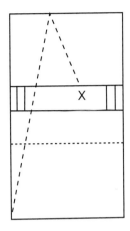

Diagram 7

Picture 9

Nick Lob Serve

From the center of the service zone, the ball hits high on the front wall, then ³/₄ court deep on the sidewall before touching the ground. The ball then comes to rest close to the back wall. *(Picture 10 and diagram 8)*

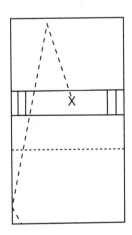

Diagram 8

Picture 10

Picture 11

Lob Z Serve

Hit from a position right of center in the service zone. The ball hits high on the front wall about 3' from the ceiling and 2' from the corner, the side wall, bounces close to the receiving line (the broken line parallel to the short line), then goes deep to the opposite side wall and drops at the back wall crack to create a very difficult return. *(Pictures 11 & 12 and diagram 9)*

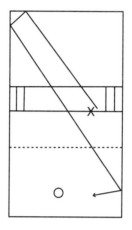

Diagram 9

Another way to hit the lob Z serve is with the backhand, which gives the serve a wider angle. *(Diagram 10)*

Picture 12

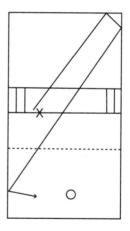

Diagram 10

3/4 Lob Z Serve

Served from right of center in the service zone and hits 3/4 up on the front wall, 1' – 2' from the corner, bounces close to the receiving line and goes deep to the opposite side, and drops close to the back wall crack.

CHAPTER 7

RETURN OF SERVE PHILOSOPHY AND TECHNIQUE

Do you have a return of serve philosophy or do you just return your opponent's serves without any plan, thought or strategy? The professionals we interviewed all use serve return strategies and we believe you should also.

Both Cliff Swain and Dan Obremski believe in varying serve returns. Dan further suggests that you try to vary the speeds at which your ball returns. Sudsy Monchik's goal is to take his opponent out of center court. Mike Yellen suggests that you be as offensively minded as possible in returning serves, provided you are winning the rallies. If you are not winning the rallies, he suggests that you go to hitting ceiling shots. Cliff Swain further recommends being aggressive on your returns, going to the opponents backhand frequently. Andy Robert's strategy is to land the ball deep into backcourt and not try to kill it. Woody Clouse suggests that if you are balanced, then hit a shot that will force your opponent off balance, otherwise, go to the ceiling. Tim Doyle returns serves according to the serve hit and its execution level. But no matter what, he says to be aggressive.

We believe in forcing the opponent out of center court as being the primary objective. An aggressive down the line pass shot or crosscourt pass can be very effective when used in the correct situations. A hard pass to the opponent's backhand is very effective, especially if you aggressively cut the ball off out of the air (without stepping into the no kill safety zone) or short hop it off the floor. If you cannot get a good aggressive return shot set-up or are off balance, then hit an effective ceiling shot trying not to hit a side wall or bring it off the back wall. If you notice your opponent loafing and not returning to center court, then an aggressive crosscourt pass shot or pinch shot can be most effective. Remember, move your opponent out of center court as aggressively as possible and into one of the back corners and take center court. If your serve is effective, then you may score the point outright, force the opponent to take an off balance shot which should give you a good set-up shot as you should now have center court position, or at a minimum you are now in the rally.

Picture 1

RETURN OF SERVE

Stay low.
Stay on the balls of your feet.
Stay forward.
(Picture 1)

RETURN OF SERVE TO YOUR FOREHAND

Move 1: A quick, short step with your right foot to point it toward the sidewall. *(Picture 2)*

Move 2: Your left foot comes across as your body turns and your racquet comes up, ready to hit. *(Picture 3)*

With these quick, two-step movements, you should be able to get to a ball on either side, all the way to the sidewall. *(Picture 4)*

Picture 2

Picture 3

Picture 4

RETURN OF SERVE TO YOUR BACKHAND

MOVE 1: A quick, short-step with the left foot to point it toward the sidewall.

This is almost a pivot, except that you lift the foot an inch off the floor and move it slightly toward the sidewall.

MOVE 2: Your right foot comes across toward the sidewall. At the same time,

Your hips and body turn and your racquet is up and back. You are ready to strike the ball.

(Pictures 5, 6, 7, and 8)

Picture 5

Picture 6

Picture 7

Picture 8

Picture 9

RETURN OF SERVE STRATEGY

As the player in the deep court, your goal is to move your opponent out of the center and into deep court so that you can move up and maintain center court position. You want to do that because you can make a much higher percentage shot from up front.

Cut Off Return of Serve

This is an offensive shot used against a lob or half lob serve. The receiver steps up and cuts off the ball in the air *(Picture 9)* or just after it bounces and hits it past the server just as they exit the service box. It is used to keep the server off balance and make them retreat quickly to the back court.

Down the Line Return of Serve

This is a high percentage shot that can drive your opponent back and to the side, so that you can take center court position. *(Picture 10 and diagram 1)*

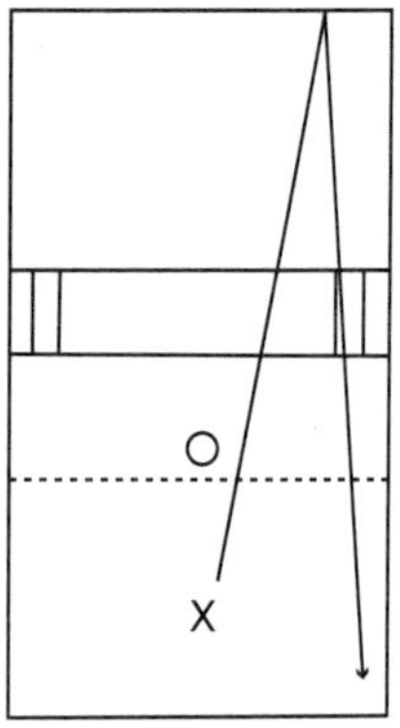

Cross Court Return of Serve

Also a high percentage shot because it can hit 18" – 20" high on the front wall. The crosscourt shot should force your opponent back so that you can move around the opposite way and take center court position. *(Picture 11 and diagram 2)*

Ceiling Return of Serve

This is a shot that is taken from deep court when you are off balance or have to return a very high serve that you can't effectively kill, shoot down the line or cross court. Keep the ceiling shot off the sidewall. It should bounce and fall deep in the backcourt without coming off the back wall. *(Picture 12 and diagram 3)*

Kill & Pinch

A more difficult shot from the deep court than the other shots. Hit a kill or pinch when the serve comes off the back wall or comes up short at three-quarter court. *(Picture 13 and diagram 4)*

Picture 10

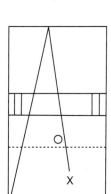

Diagram 1

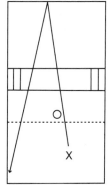

Picture 11

Diagram 2

Picture 12

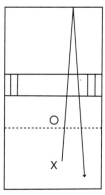

Diagram 3

Picture 13

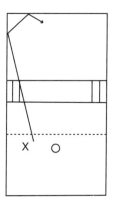

Diagram 4

CHAPTER 8

HOW TO PRESSURE YOUR OPPONENT

Have you ever heard, "You are only as good as the pressure that is put on you?" Well, that is true. When you play someone who does not put much pressure on you, it seems easier to make your shots. Your shots do not have to be quite as good. If you play against someone who puts you on the defensive much of the game, you seem to be more off balance and may have a harder time executing the shot you want to hit. There are two types of pressure; offensive pressure and defensive pressure. The pressure exerted with the ball is offensive pressure. Players should exert offensive pressure whenever possible. However, your shot strategy will change based on your opponent's strengths and weaknesses. For example, if your opponent is slow and out of shape, you may want to hit more passing shots to keep him/her running on the court. If your opponent is fast and in good condition, it is important to gain control of the center court and kill the ball. As a player, you have several choices in each rally. Try not to skip the ball as that is called an unforced error. Keep the ball in play by hitting a high percentage pass from the backcourt. Keep the ball high on the front wall, keeping your opponent moving toward the back and stretching for the ball. If you and your opponent are side by side, a pass shot is also a high percentage offensive shot moving your opponent back. (Picture 1) High percentage kill shots are generally hit when you are in the frontcourt and your opponent is in the back. You can also keep the pressure on by cutting the ball off on a fly when your opponent is in the backcourt. When you cut the ball off in the air, it is usually a surprise to your opponent. By the time they react to your cut-off, it is usually too late to retrieve the shot. (Picture 2)

Picture 1

Picture 2

Picture 3

Picture 4

The receiver on the serve performs another type of cut-off shot. The receiver should turn and be positioned to cut off lob serves. Again, this immediately puts your opponent on the defensive in the service box. *(Picture 3)* The ball, if cut-off, is hit by the server as a down the line or wide-angle pass shot. After several pass shot cut-offs, the server will be on his/her heels moving back. That is when the receiver can short-hop or cut-off the lob serve into a pinch, which will make the server move forward. Keep the offensive pressure on your opponent by moving your feet, getting into position and hitting a crisp high percentage attack shot.

Defensive pressure is the pressure exerted without the ball. Defensive pressure accounts for winning many games. Players who exert defensive pressure have a good sense of the court. You should make your opponent aware that you can hit most of the shots. Also make your opponent know that you can anticipate their shots. Stay close to your opponent, as he/she will feel your presence, which keeps the pressure on them to make the shot. *(Picture 4)* After he/she feels your pressure, you can move forward. Your anticipation of their shot is a key element to keep the pressure on. For example, if they were stretching back and off balance in the back corner, their only shot would just be to make the front wall with the ball. Therefore, by anticipating this, you should be moving up front before the ball even arrives. Stay in good position so your opponent realizes you are going to return most of their shots. This defensive pressure will force your opponent to try to make their shots better.

CHAPTER 9
DOUBLES

Doubles is a game many players enjoy playing. Doubles seems to be growing in popularity and here are a few reasons why.

1. Friendships develop as players compete and socialize afterwards.

2. Students and adults become interested because they only need to cover half of the court.

3. By playing one side of the court, your backhand or forehand (whichever side you cover) will greatly improve.

4. It is fast paced up front which makes you rely on your reflexes.

5. You will gain an awareness of movement on the court to better your court position in front of your opponent.

6. Playing with someone who understands your game will complement your style of play.

7. A team building confidence will develop between you and your partner.

HOW TO PLAY DOUBLES

The rules of doubles are similar to those of singles. However, there are a few differences. There are two players in the serving area. While one player serves, their partner must stand in the box against either sidewall. At the beginning of the game, the first team serving allows only one player to serve. When that player loses the serve, the opposing team begins their service. When the second team begins their service, both players may serve and continue in the same manner with two persons serving for each team until the game has ended. The order of service may only change between games.

On the serve in amateur play when two serves are permitted, if a player hits their partner while they are in the service box, a second serve is awarded. If they are hit on the second serve, a handout or side-out is awarded. When one serve is used, (open play) a handout or side-out is awarded. In professional play, a handout or side-out is also awarded. Other than the serving rules, all other rules in doubles are the same as in singles.

Players who are in the serving box should always move back toward the center 5' line to get into position to maintain good center court position. Each player moving from the service box should remember to wait until the flight of the ball crosses the back service line before moving out of the service box. The player in the serving box against the wall needs to move diagonally back toward the 5' line.

Picture 1

Basic Formations

Side-By-Side – Most players use a side-by side formation. The formation allows players to cover for each other when one is out of position. Each player is generally responsible to cover his or her side. *(Pictures 1 & 2 and diagram 1)*

However, when one player is up, the other is back to cover the pass or wide angle. The strategy in doubles is to make sure you are the team that covers the front of the court most of the time. Players who secure the front will generally win the match. Swings are quicker and shorter up front as the action is fast. In the backcourt, more of a full swing can be taken. *(Picture 3 and diagram 2)*

Picture 2

Picture 3

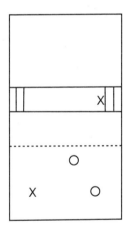

Diagram 2

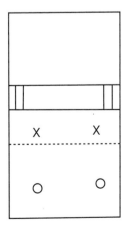

Diagram 1

"I" Formation – This formation is sometimes used. The player in the front usually has fast hands, but is slower than the back player. The player in the back is usually quicker and can cover more of the court. The deep player needs to cover corner to corner in the backcourt. *(Picture 4 and diagram 3)*

Picture 4

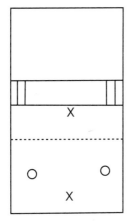

Diagram 3

Serve – The serve in doubles is very important to the serving team. You need to evaluate your opponents and generally serve to their weakness. You may find their weakness by trying different serves. For instance, if you are playing a lefty-righty team, a good serve might be a drive straight in between them.

Or you might want to hit a jam serve that comes between your opponents. A jam serve can be done with varying speeds. Try different serves until you find one that works. *(Diagrams 4 & 5)*

Serve Returns – As the serve is critical for the serving team, the return is equally important for the receiving team. Remember, the team in the frontcourt has the best advantage. Therefore, the receiving team needs to push the ball deep in the court. There are several ways this can be done. First, always take a high percentage offensive shot if possible, such as a wide-angle pass or a down-the-line pass. *(Diagrams 6 & 7)*

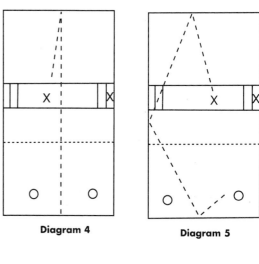

Diagram 4   **Diagram 5**

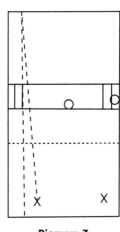

Diagram 6   **Diagram 7**

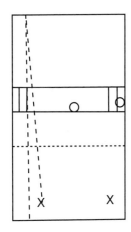

Diagram 8

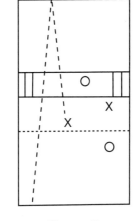

Diagram 9

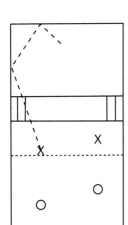

Diagram 10

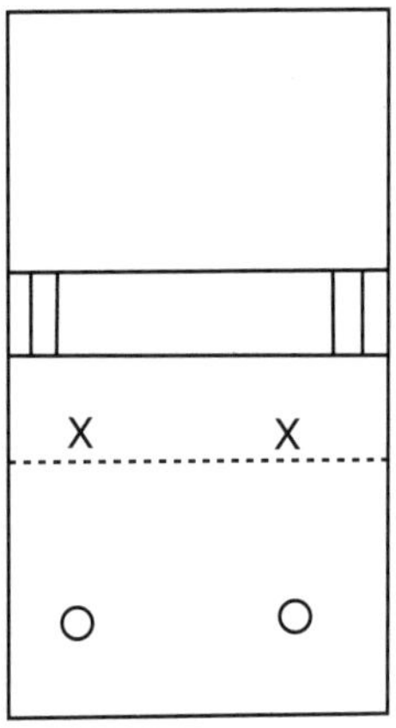

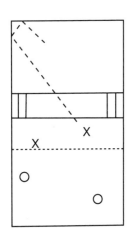

Diagram 12

These shots are high percentage because they are not kills, but pass approximately 1' – 18" high on the front wall, forcing your opponents back in the court so your team can move up. If these are not possible, then you can hit a defensive high percentage return, such as a ceiling shot. *(Diagram 8)*

Points are usually acquired when players are out of position. For example, if players are playing too far forward or if players are pushed to one side of the court, a pass is usually the best shot. *(Diagram 9)*

If you can catch one or two players too deep in the court, a pinch shot can win the rally. *(Diagram 10)*

You need to watch your opponents and play to their weakness, as well as their court position. Always remember to maintain center court position and try to stay in front of your opponents. *(Diagram 11)*

Shooting the ball from the frontcourt is much easier than in the back. You will be more accurate up front because it is a higher percentage shot. *(Diagram 12)*

Diagram 11

CHAPTER 10

ROLE MODELS

Every professional racquetball player we surveyed had a person to whom they looked up to as they were learning the game. For Mike Yellen, it was Charlie Brumfield, who according to Mike was master of the mind game. For Cliff Swain, his role model was Dave Peck, who inspired Cliff to play hard and do whatever it took to win.

Dan Obremsky listed two favorite role models, Al Plummer and Brett Harnett. Both players taught him the fighter instinct and honesty.

Mike Yellen not only had a role model, as previously mentioned, but also serves as a role model to one of our surveyed professionals, Andy Roberts. Andy commented to us that he looks up to Mike as he is always on balance when he takes a shot. Sudsy Monchik's role model was Ruben Gonzales, who is one of the greatest players of all time.

Cheryl Gudinas said this when asked who her role model was, "Not a tough one to figure out for me…Michael Jordan. What better example of hard work, dedication and mental toughness. Watching Michael over the years reminded me always of how you have to stay strong mentally and stay focused on the task at hand. He teaches those around him how to remain calm amidst utter chaos."

Cheryl says, "The person I admired most in racquetball would have to be Lynn Adams. Some argue that Michelle Gould was the best ever, but Michelle has a lot of natural strength and a booming serve. Lynn maybe didn't have the booming serve, but would always be able to find a way to get the job done, wearing her opponents down with high percentage shot selection and mental toughness. Lynn always said: "If I am down 0-10 in a game to 11, I always know that, if I can just get to three, that I am right in the game." What a great attitude!

Cheryl also admires Ruben Gonzalez. "One of my goals is to remain fit and healthy enough to play the

game at a high level longer than anyone. I try to work as hard as I think Ruben must work to stay at the competitive level he is, still winning championships against the young guys at 50. Watching Ruben, I think that, if I work harder than I think anyone else is working and take care of any ailments that may come up and combine that with Michael Jordan's and Lynn Adams' mental toughness, that will be a winning combination."

Tim Doyle insists that Larry Bird and Magic Johnson made a lasting impression on him, as they played hard every night. They also shared a mutual respect for the game and for each other.

As these professionals acknowledge, we all need a solid and reputable role model to look up to. The person or persons who can teach and inspire us to new and greater play may be a professional player, a teacher we've had in class, a coach or a friend we know and trust to give us good advice. However, it is smart to be selective in the choice of role model, as there are instances when bad players may influence us. For instance, if a well-known professional many people look up to was observed faking an injury in order to humiliate his opponent, who was clearly injured on a previous play. His only intent was to make fun of his opponent. This was an example of poor sportsmanship and is not a behavior that one wants to emulate.

Tom and I both became better players by learning from teacher coaches who became our role models. There were two people who helped me develop and learn racquetball. Pat Casey was my first mentor, who spent many hours playing, lecturing and drilling me into becoming a better player. I'll never forget Pat's unselfish attitude of playing me for several years without complaint, patiently beating up on me, knowing that I did not have the skill to compete on the same level as he. Because Pat never gave up on me, combined with my stubborn attitude, I slowly became a competitive player. The second role model who influenced my life is Tom Travers, my co-author. Tom's knowledge of racquetball mechanics astounded me and his ability to communicate these principals is highly successful. Tom's major impact on my life was his attitude of always being willing to share his knowledge of racquetball with others and me, even though we often compete against each other.

Tim is absolutely correct in explaining the importance of role models in influencing our lives. I have two important role models, Marty Hogan and Cliff Swain. Marty was the first player ever to win more professional titles than anyone else. Marty's training and conditioning enabled him to play power racquetball using a racquet that is half the size of today's racquets. Cliff Swain has won more titles than any other professional. Cliff also left racquetball for several years, only to make a comeback and regain his championship professional title. Cliff is small in stature compared to many other professionals, but his tenacity and mental toughness enabled him to regain his title against great odds.

As players, we need to pick out one or two aspects of our role models game that helps us improve. For me, it was Marty Hogan's power and Cliff Swain's mental toughness, which I've tried to emulate. I used my inspiration from Cliff Swain to learn to win within myself by practicing every shot until I mastered each of them. Learning to improve every shot develops the confidence to become a champion.

So find yourself a positive role model with high standards. The following are some guidelines that will assist you in choosing a role model.

1. Seek a person who is honest, with high integrity. They should have a genuine concern for others and demonstrate a sincere interest in making you a better player.

2. Find a teacher or coach who emphasizes correct mechanics. Ask people at your club to identify the best instructors and get references from players they have taught. Expect to pay for these services. If you find a good instructor, it is worth the money.

3. Look for an instructor with patience and one who is committed to you achieving your goals. Don't hesitate to cancel the lessons if you don't see improvement in your game after several lessons. Do give the instructor a chance to improve your skills, as it does take time, patience and practice.

4. Pattern your game after a role model with proven tournament experience, but remember not all good players are good teachers and not all good teachers were professional tour players.

5. Teach yourself to play better by watching experienced role models play. Go to amateur and professional tournaments and study the best players looking for ways to improve your game. As you watch these players, ask yourself "What mechanics do they use when taking certain shots? How do they position themselves in order to achieve maximum advantage of their court position? What type of game strategy are they employing?"

CHAPTER II

MENTAL CONCENTRATION, IMAGERY AND ATTITUDE

Cliff Swain believes that "mental toughness" will win more matches than any other aspect of the game. He also challenges us to be well rounded with strength, speed, and solid forehand and backhand, good serves and returns, power and touch. Mike Yellen and Dan Obremsky feel that the mental part of racquetball is the most important part of the game. Sudsy Monchik keeps his mental strategy simple stating, "Play hard and have fun!" Adam Karp articulates the need to never lose focus. Jason Mannino believes that mental toughness is closely associated with visualization. Jason says to stay positive, visualize your opponent's strengths and weaknesses, visualize your habits, and then use this information to visualize what works against your opponent. What is mental toughness and how do we incorporate it into our game? Mental toughness is an attitude. It's the desire to use your mind to concentrate on particular shots or situations to find a way to win. Cheryl Gudinas feels like she is never out of a game no matter what the score is. Mental toughness is the ability to reach down inside ourselves and find that extra effort that enables us to gain an edge over many of our opponents. Mental toughness can be learned and improved through learning to concentrate, developing mental imagery, having a positive attitude and developing a desire to never give up. The following is a more detailed description of these aspects of mental toughness:

1. **Concentration** – is the ability to keep your mind focused throughout a point, a game and a match. In order to concentrate, you must first try to rid yourself of unnecessary distractions. Forget the bad call a referee made, don't worry about a prelim at work, or think about that fight you had with a friend or a spouse. Next, ensure that you are watching the ball everywhere it goes on the court. Make sure you know where your opponent is positioned on the court at all times. Don't worry so much about the score, although you should know it, but play all out on every point concentrating on scoring one point at a time. Also, before a match begins, you should already have a game plan of what you want to accomplish. If you stick with a strategy already established, then you won't need to make many adjustments during the match. This should permit you more time to focus on the rally you are engaged in.

2. **Mental Imagery** – is a technique that many athletes use to improve their concentration by picturing in their mind an image of them actually playing out a point, game and then the match. This technique works best when you are in a relaxed mood, with no observable distractions. To use this technique, you would imagine you're in a match with an upcoming opponent and you play the match out in your head, envisioning the shots you would take in certain situations, picking apart your opponent's weaknesses, playing out each point from beginning to end. Using this technique, you could imagine yourself in a tiebreaker with you using certain strategies to ensure you win that last point. You can also pretend you are playing in a match with several tough rallies, asking yourself what worked and what action resulted in your opponent scoring a point. Then you replay the point using a strategy that will ensure success. The advantages to using metal imagery include:

   A. It is a fun and relaxing way to kill some time.

   B. Mental imagery has helped many players become better players by preparing them mentally for what to expect of certain opponents.

   C. It doesn't cost you anything but time!

   D. The technique can help you to relax much the same as meditation works for some people, as you need to place all distractions out of your mind and meditate (concentrate) on your imagery.

The only disadvantage to this technique would be if you did not know your opponents' strengths and weaknesses and prepared mentally with wrong information, then you will probably play accordingly.

3. **Positive Attitude** – It is absolutely imperative that you keep a positive attitude on the court. Most people who play racquetball are constantly talking to themselves as they play. This talk can either be of a positive or negative nature. Most successful player reinforce the positive by saying things like, "nice try," "I'll get that next time," "turn your feet toward the wall next time and you'll make that shot," "get your elbow up and you ace that forehand," etc. Also, when you make a good shot give yourself credit by saying "excellent kill," "way to concentrate," "nice touch," etc. If you talk in this manner, you'll be surprised at the improvement in your game. Players who constantly say or think negatively such as, "you idiot," "That stinks," "he's too strong for me," "I'll never beat this person," or "you stupid #$%@!," then you'll probably end up beating yourself.

Also, if the same person consistently beats you, don't give up—find out why! Are they better skilled than you? Then you should find a good mechanics coach to improve your skills. Are you equal in ability and skill level? Try to improve your concentration techniques, develop a better game plan, relax and try not to over-play or play with more intensity. Another good idea is to video tape your matches and watch for weakness in both yourself and your opponent. Improve on your inconsistencies and exploit your opponents. If you have tried everything and are still losing, then take some time off from playing this person. It may just be a mental block that only time off will cure.

CHAPTER 12

TRAINING

The professionals we surveyed all used different training routines that were designed specifically around their interests. However, each program also had many similarities. For example, most of our pros recommended playing or practicing racquetball for one hour a day.

The majority of the professionals augment their practice and play time with other routines. Dan Obremski goes to a step class two or three times a week and does sprints one day a week. Mike Yellen lifts weights for his upper body strength three days per week and bikes, runs or uses the Stairmaster three days per week. Cliff Swain works mainly with weights and endurance training during the pro tour season and when he does practice, he plays only one match as hard as he can. He cautions against playing four or five hours a day, which hurts your game as it forces you to play tired and lazy, developing bad habits and risking injury.

Sudsy Monchik lifts weights during the off-season and preseason and works on cardiovascular training six days a week year round. Adam Karp lifts weights and works on cardiovascular training, primarily during the off-season. Jason Mannino uses light weights with high repetitions during the off-season and during the season, he doesn't lift any weights and instead cross-trains a lot. After a pro-stop, he doesn't play for one week. Woody Clouse emphasizes making racquetball practice time a priority with strength and endurance as secondary.

Cheryl Gudinas believes that people waste their time doing workouts for racquetball that do not incorporate proper and appropriate movements of the game. She works out emphasizing strength, balance, coordination and flexibility. She cross-trains by running, cycling and rollerblading two to three times a week. She strength trains three times a week, works on speed and foot skill training one to two times a week and plays/drills five times a week.

Tim Doyle recommends sticking to a consistent routine, focusing on explosive type strength-training exercise. He rotates his strength workouts into lower body one day and upper body the next. He recommends exercise repetitions for exercise of 12 to 30 of two or three sets. This strength program allows your body to build strength and stamina. Tim believes playing racquetball only gives you a base fitness level. To achieve the maximum potential, racquetball requires short bursts of power movements over a one to two hour period. He uses ply-metrics; speed, agility and quickness drills; medicine balls and balance drills to improve his game.

We believe that training for racquetball needs to combine training variables of strength, flexibility and fitness. The following are our recommendations for training for racquetball:

WARM UP AND COOL DOWNS – A 10 minute warm-up and cool down is recommended for all exercise and practice sessions. Warm ups should be completed before any strenuous activity. A safe warm-up should include 5-10 minutes of an activity that slowly gets the cardiovascular system pumping blood to all your muscles. A slow jog, ride on an exercise bike, swimming and racquetball aerobics are examples of warm-up activities that need to be performed at a pace that progressively increases until your pace at the end of the warm-up is approximately the same pace at which you will be performing the activity. Slow stretching of all the muscles you will be using in performing the activity should follow this warm up period.

Cool downs are performed after your racquetball games or workout, but instead of increasing your pace, you slow your pace down until your heart rate is close to when you first began your warm up. Finish the cool down by stretching all the muscles you've just used in your workout.

STRENGTH TRAINING – The most important reason to strength train is to prevent injuries. When your muscles are strong, especially around a joint such as the knee, elbow, ankle or shoulder, the muscles will take the majority of the force during play instead of the much weaker tendons and ligaments supporting the joints. Also, strength training increases the size of the muscle fibers making them larger and stronger, thus enabling you to hit the ball with more force.

The best way to strength train is through use of free weights (barbells and dumbbells) or machine weights (machines designed specifically to weight train). The principles discussed in this chapter are the same for either use of free weights or machine weights and are interchangeable.

Weight training for racquetball should be done a minimum of two or three times per week on upper body muscles (muscles above the waist) and two or three times per week for lower body muscles during the off season. Any muscle group should not be worked two or more days in a row. To make this simple, you could do upper body exercises of the chest press (pectoral muscles), military press (deltoids), lat-pull downs (latisimus dorsi muscles), bicep curls (bicep muscles), triceps extensions (triceps muscles), wrist curls (forearm flexors) and back rows (lower back muscles) on Mondays, Wednesdays and Fridays and lower body exercises of the leg extensions (quadriceps), leg curls (hamstrings), calf raises (calf muscles), squats (glutei's) and abduction exercises (abductors) and adductions exercises (adductors) on Tuesdays, Thursdays, and Saturdays. During the racquetball tournament season, weight training should continue at least one time per week minimum and preferably two times per week on each muscle group.

In your weight-training program, we recommend completing three sets of ten repetitions for each major muscle group. This program is recommended to increase strength and endurance (the ability of the muscles to perform over an extended period of time). It is a safe yet effective way to weight train. To determine your starting weight for each exercise, you must determine the amount of weight you can lift for 10 repetitions (this means you can not lift this weight for an 11th repetition). Once you determine this starting weight for all upper body and lower body exercise, your first set of each exercise will include completing 10 repetitions of 1/2 (50%) of the exercises starting weight. The next set will involve your completing 10 repetitions of 3/4 (75%) of the starting weight. The final set you should lift as many repetitions as you are able at the starting weight (100%). When you can perform all three sets of 10 repetitions at these weights you should increase your weight by 5 lbs. – 10 lbs. the next time you workout. An example of this weight training method for the bench press would have a person able to press 100 lbs. a maximum of 10 repetitions. Since he/she cannot get this weight up for the 11th repetition, he/she knows they are at the correct starting weight. He/she would then perform one set of 10 repetitions at 50 lbs., a second set of 10 at 75 lbs., and a third set at 100 lbs. completing as many repetitions as he/she is able to. Again, when he/she completes all 10 repetitions on the last set, he/she will raise the weight 5 or 10 lbs. the next time he/she works out.

An example of a weekly program for the off-season is as follows:

UPPER BODY PROGRAM (WEEK 1)

Exercises	Monday		Wednesday		Friday	
Bench Press	Set 1	10 x 50 lbs.	Set 1	10 x 50 lbs.	Set 1	10 x 50 lbs.
100 lbs.	Set 2	10 x 75 lbs.	Set 2	10 x 75 lbs.	Set 2	10 x 75 lbs.
Starting wt.	Set 3	7 x 100 lbs.	Set 3	8 x 100 lbs.	Set 3	10 x 100 lbs.

Picture 1

Picture 2

1. Bench Press *(Pictures 1 and 2)*

   a. Lie on a bench with your back flat.

   b. Hold the bar over your chest with your arms extended.

   c. Lower the bar to your chest slowly and under control.

   d. Press/push the bar to the starting position.

Muscle groups targeted: Pectoralis major, deltoids, triceps

Proceed to complete three sets of the following upper body exercises on Mondays, Wednesdays and Fridays (same pattern as demonstrated in Exercise 1-Bench Press).

2. Military Press *(Pictures 3 and 4)*

   a. Using free weights or a weight machine, sit or stand with the weight bar under the chin and shoulder height.

   b. Lift the bar over the head until the arms are fully extended.

   c. Slowly lower the bar to the starting position.

Muscle groups targeted: Deltoids and triceps

3. Lat Pull Downs *(Pictures 5 and 6)*

   a. Select proper weight.

   b. Connect the bar to the overhead cable on a lat pull down machine.

   c. Grab the bar with the hands in the grips.

   d. Pull the bar down until it is chest high.

   e. Slowly return the weight to the starting position.

Muscle groups targeted: Latissimus, trapezius, bicep and deltoid

Picture 3

Picture 4

Picture 5

Picture 6

Picture 7

Picture 8

Picture 9

Picture 10

Picture 11

4. Back Rows *(Pictures 7 and 8)*

   a. Attach a row bar to the cable of a row machine.

   b. Select appropriate weight.

   c. Grab the row bar with the arms extended, while in a seated position with the legs slightly bent.

   d. Pull the bar back to your stomach.

   e. Slowly extend the bar back to the starting position.

Muscle groups targeted: Latissimus dorsi, trapezius teres major and minor

5. Bicep Curls *(Picture 9)*

   a. Start with arms extended and the hands holding dumbbells at your sides.

   b. Lift the dumbbells to chest height.

   c. Slowly lower the dumbbells to the starting position.

Muscles groups targeted: Biceps

6. Triceps Extensions *(Picture 10)*

   a. Support the upper body by holding on to a bench for support.

   b. With the opposite hand, hold a dumbbell in a slightly curled position.

   c. Extend the dumbbell backwards until the arm is slightly straight.

   d. Return the dumbbell to the starting position.

Muscle groups targeted: Triceps

7. Wrist Curls *(Picture 11)*

   a. Sit and hold a dumbbell in one hand that is supported on your leg.

   b. Curl the hand upwards as far a possible, pausing for a second.

   c. Slowly lower the dumbbell until the hand is fully extended.

Muscle groups targeted: Forearm flexors

LOWER BODY AND STOMACH MUSCLES (WEEK 1)

Exercises	Tuesday		Thursday		Saturday	
Leg Extension	Set 1	10 x 80 lbs.	Set 1	10 x 80 lbs.	Set 1	10 x 80 lbs.
160 lbs starting	Set 2	10 x 120 lbs.	Set 2	10 x 120 lbs.	Set 2	10 x 120 lbs.
wt. Two legs	Set 3	6 x 160 lbs.	Set 3	8 x 160 lbs.	Set 3	10 x 160 lbs.

Picture 13

1. Leg Extensions *(Pictures 13 and 14)*

a. Select weight.

b. Start in a seated position with the feet placed under weight pad.

c. Extend the legs until they are straight and parallel with the floor.

d. Slowly lower the weight back to the starting position.

Picture 14

Muscle groups targeted: Quadriceps

Proceed to complete three sets of the following lower body and stomach exercises on Tuesdays, Thursdays and Saturdays (same pattern Demonstrated in exercise 1. Leg-Extensions).

2. Leg Curls *(Pictures 15 and 16)*

a. Select weight.

b. Lie on the leg curl machine with your stomach flat and your heels under the weight pad.

c. Lift the weight pad back until you touch your buttocks.

d. Slowly lower the weight back to the starting position.

Picture 15

Muscle groups targeted: Hamstrings, gluteals

3. Calf Raises *(Pictures 17 and 18)*

a. Set your weight.

b. Slowly raise the feet up by standing on your toes as far as possible.

c. Slowly lower the feet until the heels are as low as they go.

d. Raise the feet back to the starting position.

Picture 16

Muscle groups used: Gastrocnemius, soleus

Picture 17   **Picture 18**

Picture 19

Picture 20

Picture 21

Picture 22

Picture 23

Picture 24

4. Squats *(Pictures 19 and 20)*

   a. Select your weight.

   b. Raise the barbell or weight bar until it rests on your shoulders.

   c. Place your feet shoulder width apart.

   d. Slowly lower the bar until you are in a seated position with the knees bent, until they are parallel with the floor.

   e. Straighten the legs until you are in the start position.

Muscle groups targeted: Quadriceps, hamstrings, and gastrocnemius

5. Stomach (Abdominal) Machine *(Pictures 21 and 22)*

   a. Select weight and adjust weight pad bar.

   b. Push the stomach machine weight pad forward by contracting the stomach (abdominal) muscles.

   c. Slowly lower the weight pad back to the starting position.

Muscle groups targeted: Abdominals

6. Side Twist *(Pictures 23 and 24)*

   a. Select your weight, sit in machine and place arms in the proper position.

   b. Keeping the chest and hips facing forward, twist the weight pad to the side.

   c. Slowly return the weight pad back to the starting position.

   d. After the set is complete, repeat these steps toward the opposite side.

Muscle groups targeted: Obliques, abdominals

7. Hip Machines

Abduction Exercise #1 *(Pictures 25 and 26)*

   a. Select weight, sit on machine, secure seatbelt and arrange weight pads facing out.

   b. Push the weight pads outward (away from the body) as far as possible.

   c. Slowly return the weight pads to the starting position.

Muscle groups targeted: Gluteus medius, gluteus minimus

Adduction Exercise #2 *(Pictures 27 and 28)*

   a. Select weight, sit on machine, secure seatbelt and arrange weight pads facing inward.

   b. Adjust machine so the weight pad is pulled toward the body.

   c. Pull the legs and pads toward the middle as far as possible.

   d. Slowly return the weight pads to the starting position.

Muscle groups targeted: Adductors, gracilis

You may want to change your weight-training program whenever you have reached a plateau and are no longer improving muscular strength or you wish to concentrate more on muscular endurance. To increase muscular strength, attempt lifting less repetitions and more weight. For example, instead of bench-pressing 3 sets of 10 repetitions at 50 lbs., 75 lbs., and 100 lbs., lift 3 sets of 5 repetitions at 60 lbs. 85lbs.and 110 lbs. Should you want to improve muscular endurance, attempt lifting more repetitions and less weight. For example, instead of completing leg extensions of 3 sets of 10 repetitions at 100 lbs., 150 lbs., and 200 lbs., lift 3 sets of 15 repetitions at 80 lbs., 130 lbs., and 180 lbs.

Additional strength training principals include:

   1. Breathing when lifting. Always breathe in (inhale) and out (exhale) on every repetition. An easy way to remember to breathe properly is "breathe in" when lifting the weight toward the body and "blow it away" when extending the weight away from the body.

   2. Speed of repetitions. Usually, it is better to slowly lift the weight during the contraction phase of a weight repetition, i.e. "one thousand one, one thousand two," and then slowly extend the weight to a count of "one,

Picture 25

Picture 26

Picture 27

Picture 28

two, three, four." Occasionally, you may wish to use lighter weights and speed up the repetitions to a fast count to assist with developing fast twitch muscles fibers. However, to increase strength and develop the whole muscle it is best to lift slowly and under control.

3. Keep a weight training record chart that includes the exercise, date, and number of sets, resistance, and repetitions. Set goals that are difficult, yet achievable.

4. During the competitive season when you no longer have the time to lift each muscle group 3 times per week, attempt to strength train each muscle group at least 1 time per week to maintain strength. Also, during the competitive season, you may wish to strength train muscles more specifically for racquetball with stability and medicine balls and light dumbbells as mentioned in this next section.

STRENGTH TRAINING WITH A STABILITY BALL AND MEDICINE BALL

We asked World Champion, Cheryl Gudinas, to share a favorite workout routine she uses specifically for racquetball.

Cheryl uses a stability ball, dumbbells and a medicine ball to do strength-training routines on a racquetball court. Each set should be repeated 15 times.

The first routine is used to strengthen the hamstring and abdominal muscles.

1. Hamstring Raise *(Picture 29)*
   a. Place your heels on the stability ball.

   b. Place hands to sides for support.

   c. Raise the hips and straighten the legs and hold for two seconds.

2. Hamstring Curl *(Picture 30)*
   a. Place heel on the stability ball.

   b. Place hands to sides for support.

   c. Raise the hips and straighten the legs.

   d. Curl the ball toward the body.

Picture 29

Picture 30

3. Abdominal Crunches (straight) *(Pictures 31 and 32)*

a. Sit on a stability ball and hold a medicine ball in front of the chest.

b. Lay back on the ball.

c. Return to the starting position by tightening the stomach muscles.

4. Abdominal Crunches (Twist) *(Picture 33, 34 and 35)*

a. Lay back on stability ball and hold the medicine ball in front of the chest.

b. Tighten the stomach muscle and raise your upper body to a sitting position.

c. Twist to the right side then twist to the left side.

5. Leg Press *(Pictures 36 and 37)*

a. Lay with your back flat on the floor.

b. Place hands under the back for support.

c. Hold the utility ball between the feet.

d. Pull knees toward the chest then extend legs straight out and hold for two seconds.

6. Abdominal Roll Outs *(Picture 38)*

a. Start with the hand placed on the top of the utility ball, knees on the floor, back straight.

b. Slowly roll forward on your forearms.

c. Slowly roll back to the starting position.

Picture 31

Picture 32

Picture 33

Picture 34

Picture 35

Picture 36

Picture 37

Picture 38

Picture 39

Picture 40

Picture 41

Picture 42

Picture 43

Picture 44

7. **Chest Fly's** *(Pictures 39 and 40)*

   a. Lay with upper back supported on the utility ball.

   b. Extend arms straight and hold a pair of dumbbells directly over chest.

   c. Lower the dumbbells to the sides until the arms are straight and horizontal with the floor.

   d. Pull dumbbells toward the start position directly over the chest.

8. **One Legged Squat** *(Pictures 41 and 42)*

   a. Hold the ball against the wall with your back. One foot is planted flat on the floor and the other foot is held out in front of the body.

   b. Slowly lower yourself by bending one knee, while keeping the other straight out and lifted off the floor. Squat to a position whereby the bent knee is at a 90° angle to the floor.

   c. Return to starting position.

9. **Bicep Curl** *(Pictures 43 and 44)*

   a. Sit on the stability ball with one leg on the floor for balance.

   b. Arms are extended straight and to the side.

   c. Bring dumbbells upward to the shoulder by contracting the bicep muscles.

   d. Slowly lower the dumbbells to the start position.

10. Stationary Lunge (1 Leg) *(Picture 45 and 46)*

   a. Take one foot and place it on the stability ball behind you, front leg is slightly bent and hands are on hips.

   b. Slowly bend the front leg until its 90° angle to the floor while stretching the quadriceps muscle of the back leg. Hold that position for two seconds.

   c. Return to the starting position.

11. Russian Twists (Abdominals and Obliques *(Pictures 47, 48, 49, and 50)*

   a. With the back supported on the stability ball, arms straight and extended, hold the medicine ball at chest level.

   b. Twist to one side.

   c. Return to start position.

   d. Twist to opposite side.

Picture 45   **Picture 46**

Picture 47

Picture 48

Picture 49

Picture 50

FITNESS TRAINING

Racquetball is a very strenuous activity that requires the player to be physically fit. Racquetball requires both aerobic and anaerobic conditioning. The aerobic conditioning (breathing continuously through-out the exercise) is best obtained by working out at a steady level that is over your minimum target heart rate level, yet does not go over your maximum level, for at least 20-40 minutes. This type of exercise program should be done at least five times per week during the off-season and three times per week during the season. This target heart rate is the level to which you should raise your heart rate during exercise in order to receive an aerobic conditioning effect. Sports and workouts such as swimming, jogging, bicycling, step aerobics, treadmill running, cross country skiing, and racquetball, all assist with improving cardiovascular fitness and this desired aerobic training effect. The heart rate can be calculated in a safe and accurate way to assess whether you are working at the intensity necessary for healthy conditioning for your age group. The heart rate can be calculated by using the following formula; 220 – Age x 60% to calculate your minimum heart rate; 220 – Age x 80%, to calculate your maximum heart rate. An example of how to use this formula correctly would have a person 30 years old would need to work out for at least 20 minutes at a heart rate between 114 minimum

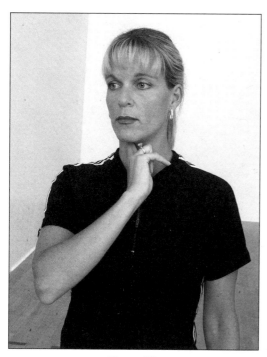

Picture 50

and 162 maximum. It is important to get your heart rate over 114 (60% of your recommended maximum heart rate) in order to receive benefit from your exercise, yet you do not want to go over 162 (maximum recommended heart rate), which would make you tire to quickly and may be dangerous.

The best training effect for aerobic conditioning will be achieved if you keep your heart rate in the range of 60-80% of the exercise heart rate chart for the 20 – 40 minute workout.

To determine your heart rate, place two fingers along the carotid artery in your neck and count every time you feel a pulse for one minute. *(Picture 50)*

For your convenience, we have provided you with the following heart rate exercise chart with the minimum and maximum heart rates already calculated.

EXERCISE HEART RATE CHART

AGE	20	25	30	35	40	45	50	55	60	65	
MIN	120	117	114	111	108	105	102	99	96	93	60%
MAX	170	166	162	157	153	149	145	140	136	132	80%

Racquetball also requires a great amount of anaerobic conditioning (exercise that requires a one breath and an all out effort) as there is a great deal of all out effort exerted to play out a point with little time to breath rhythmically. We recommend sprints of at least 40 yards or more for anaerobic training.

CIRCUIT TRAINING

An excellent way to train for racquetball that combines strength training and cardiovascular conditioning is to circuit train (alternate stations).

A good program of circuit training would include 5 minutes on a cardiovascular machine (an exercise bike, treadmill, rowing machine, step machine, jump rope, etc.) so that the target heart rate is in the range of 70% - 80%. Next, use a set of weights or a weight machine (bench press, military press, leg extension, etc.) to complete three sets of 10 repetitions, with as little rest time between sets as possible. Then rotate to a cardiovascular machine and exercise for another five minutes. This procedure of alternating between a cardiovascular and weight training exercise is repeated for 20 – 30 minutes of cardiovascular exercise plus the time needed for the weight training exercise. An example of a training circuit for a 20-year old person follows:

Station 1: Five minutes on a treadmill machine raising the heart rate to within the target range of 140 (70%) and 170 (80%). Repeat this intensity for all cardiovascular stations.

Station 2: Perform three sets of 10 repetitions (using the recommendations for weight training previously mentioned in this book) on the bench press. Rotate to the next station as quickly as possible.

Station 3: Five minutes on a step machine.

Station 4: Three sets of ten repetitions of military press.

Station 5: Five minutes on an exercise bike.

Station 6: Three sets of ten repetitions lat pull-downs.

Station 7: Five minutes on a cross-country ski machine.

Station 8: Three sets of ten repetitions back rows.

Station 9: Five minutes jumping rope.

Station 10: Three sets of ten repetitions bicep curls.

Station 11: Five minutes on a rowing machine.

Station 12: Three sets of ten repetitions triceps extensions.

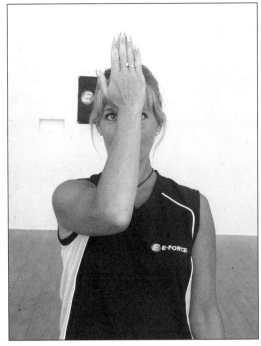

Picture 51

FLEXIBILITY

STRETCHING – An important part of a fitness and conditioning program for racquetball includes a routine that properly stretches all major muscle groups. When muscles are properly warmed up and stretched, they will perform more efficiently and be less likely to be injured. A complete list of stretching activities specifically recommended for racquetball follows:

1. Neck Stretches *(Pictures 51 and 52)*

  a. Place your hand on your forehead and apply pressure with your forehead pushing against your hand for 20-30 seconds and release.

  b. Place your hand on the back of your head and apply pressure with the back of your head against your hand for 20-30 seconds and release.

  c. Follow these same procedures and stretch the side of the neck to the right and then the left side.

Picture 52

Picture 53

Picture 54

Picture 55

Picture 56

Picture 57

Picture 58

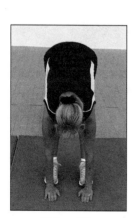

Picture 59

2. Arm and Shoulder Stretch *(Pictures 53 and 54)*

  a. Clutch your right arm at the wrist and pull it back behind the head and hold this position for at least 20-30 seconds.

  b. Proceed to do this same stretch with the left arm.

3. Lat Stretch *(Pictures 55 and 56)*

  a. Extend your arms above the head and interlock the fingers of both hands.

  b. Pull your hands down until they are below and behind the head and release your fingers.

  c. Pull your shoulders back and slowly drop your elbows until they drop to your sides. You should feel the stretch in your latisumus dorsi (lats).

4. Side Stretches *(Pictures 57 and 58)*

  a. Extend your arms over your head and interlock the fingers of your two hands

  b. Slowly stretch your whole upper body to the right side as far as you can and hold this position for at least 20-30 seconds.

  c. Repeat this same stretch to the left side.

5. Toe Touches *(Picture 59)*

  a. Bend forward at the waist and slowly extend your arms and hands toward the floor reaching as far towards the floor as possible.

  b. Hold this stretch position for at least 20-30 seconds.

  c. Repeat this stretch with the left foot crossed over the right foot.

  d. Repeat this stretch with the right foot crossed over the left foot.

6. Quadriceps Stretches *(Picture 60 and 61)*

  a. Reach back and take your right foot and pull your leg towards your buttocks, stretching your quadriceps muscle.

  b. Hold your stretch for at least 20-30 seconds. Repeat this same stretch with your opposite leg.

7. Calf Stretch *(Picture 62*

  a. Position yourself close to and facing a wall, plant your back right foot flatly on the floor, keeping the leg straight.

  b. Bend your left front knee towards the wall and lean towards the wall.

  c. Slowly stretch the right calf muscle for at least 20 seconds and release.

  d. Repeat this process with your opposite leg.

8. Inner Thigh Stretch *(Picture 63)*

  a. Sit on the floor and place the heels of your feet together.

  b. Grab your ankles with your hands, push with your elbows against your legs forcing them toward the floor with steady pressure that slowly stretches the inner thigh muscles (groin).

  c. Hold this stretch position for at least 20-30 seconds.

Picture 60

Picture 61

Picture 62

Picture 63

SPECIFIC RACQUETBALL TRAINING DRILLS

Sprints- Sprints are an excellent anaerobic conditioner that should be done at least one time per week. If a track is available, eventually work up to completing 10-40 yard sprints.

If a track is not available, try doing sprints on a racquetball court. Try to work up to 20 on-court sprints. Start with your foot touching the back wall.

  1. Sprint to the front wall touch it with your hand.

  2. Turn and sprint back.

  3. You can increase the distance you run by repeating steps 1-3 on the same sprint, i.e. Run down, back, down, back = ONE SPRINT.

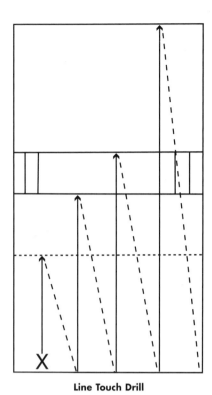

Line Touch Drill

Agility Drills- These drills are performed the same as the on-court sprints, but with different movements:

1. Skipping Steps –Skip on right leg, and then skip on the left leg. Raise knees high and glide.

2. Cross-Over Steps- Run sideways parallel with a side wall crossing the right foot over the left foot, then step left, right foot behind the left foot, step left.

3. Backward Sprint- Run backwards as fast as possible.

4. Slide Steps- Slide step sideways parallel with a sidewall with the right foot sliding sideways until it touches the left foot. Push off the right foot and slide toward the front wall.

Turn and Cuts

1. Face the back wall and run backwards at an angle to the front wall, plant one foot and change angle.

2. Continue running backwards at this new angle, still toward the front wall.

3. Repeat the process, running backwards while you are facing the front wall.

Line Touch Drill- This is another excellent quickness and conditioning drill that is performed on a racquetball court.

1. Start with one foot touching the back wall.

2. Sprint to the receiving line, touch it with one hand and sprint back to the back wall and touch it.

3. Sprint to the short line, touch it with your hand then sprint back to the back wall and touch it.

4. Sprint to the serving line, touch it and sprint to the back wall and touch it.

5. Sprint to the front wall and touch it at the base, turn and sprint back.

This completes the drill. Use a stopwatch and time the drill. With practice, the time it takes to complete the drill will improve.

Jump Rope- This is a great conditioning exercise that can be completed on a racquetball court.
(Picture 64)

To achieve your maximum potential, racquetball requires short bursts of power movements over a one or two hour period. Training in this fashion increases the level of play.

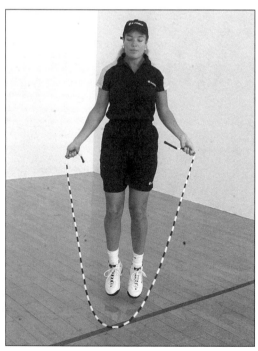

Picture 64

We asked Tim Doyle, a top professional tour player, to share a few of his favorite racquetball specific training workouts. Tim said, "To improve your racquetball game to the highest level you must train functionally or sports specific."

Jelly Ball (**Medicine Ball**)-This is Tim's favorite exercise for power and abdominal strength.

1. With the ball in a position in front of the body, pull back the medicine ball toward the right side.

2. Take the medicine ball and use the same motion as forehand serve and throw the ball toward the sidewall.

3. Do 3 sets of 10, focusing on explosion.
   (Pictures 65, 66, and 67)

4. Take the ball back as in a back hand shot.

5. Follow through in a motion that simulates taking a backhand shot and throw the ball toward the sidewall.

6. Do 3 sets of 10, focusing on explosion.
   (Pictures 68, 69, and 70)

Ply- Metrics- A 12" and 24" step box is recommended to perform the ply-metric conditioning drills. Do 3 sets of 10 repetitions.

Drill 1 – Forward Thrust

1. Get in a return of serve ready, starting position.

2. Explode forward and upward onto the top of the box, landing with both feet into a balanced ready position.

3. Jump back to the starting position.
   (Pictures 71 and 72)

Picture 65

Picture 66

Picture 67

Picture 68

Picture 69

Picture 70

Picture 71

Picture 72

Picture 73

Picture 74

Picture 75

Picture 76

Picture 77

Picture 78

Picture 79

Drill 2

1. Get in a 'return of serve' ready position with the box placed to your side.

2. Explode sideways and up, landing both feet on top of the box.

3. Jump off the box sideways into the starting position.

4. Perform the same exercise from the opposite side of the box.
   (Pictures 73 and 74)

Drill 3- Do the same drills as in 1 and 2 with one-foot hops. *(Pictures 75 and 76)*

Ladder Drills – An excellent tool to improve speed, agility, flexibility and quickness is the quick foot ladder. This ladder is laid out on the floor and has about 20 rungs. It enables participants to run, skip, jump, side step and twist. When you do the ladder drills, focus on quality of movement and speed.

Some examples of some routines you can try on a ladder include:

High Steps *(Picture 77)*

Cross Over Steps *(Picture 78)*

Back Crossover Steps *(Picture 79)*

Balancing – Racquetball requires you to hit many of your shots while moving. This is where balance and agility come into play. An effective tool for improving balance is to use agility balance discs. They are round shaped discs with tennis balls under each disc. To use a balance disc you must:

1. Get in a ready balanced position by standing on the disc.

2. Try to hold balance for one minute intervals.
   (Pictures 80 and 81)

This balance routine is effective in strengthening the stabilizing muscles of the upper legs, inner thighs and lower back.

Picture 80

Picture 81

PRACTICING AND CLASSROOM DRILLS

PRACTICING – There is absolutely no substitute for practice! The problem is most racquetball players would rather play a game than spend much needed time refining their shots, improving mechanics, developing a backhand or perfecting their serve. We believe every shot needs to be mastered to a point which you feel confident in its execution every time you use it in competition. This requires practice and more practice.

There are basically three levels of practice. The first level is when you practice by yourself, hitting practice shots off the floor, out of your hand and off the walls in a variety of places on the court. Level two is practice with a partner who takes a center court position, but who is basically inactive. Level three requires practice with a partner as an active participant who returns shots and applies game situation pressure.

Level 1

Practicing by yourself: In this level, you should first practice and perfect your forehand and backhand strokes. Before you can advance to higher levels of play, you must perfect these basic swing mechanics.

1. **Forehand and backhand drills:** Practicing the forehand is accomplished by first drilling the down the line shot. Using the mechanics we previously discussed, you hit the forehand shot by bouncing the ball off the floor and hitting it with your weight on your front foot, keeping the ball low so it caroms low off the front wall. The shot should rebound and bounce twice off the floor before it hits the back wall. Hit this shot to perfection, ensuring that it doesn't hit the sidewall, as this slows the ball down and almost always ends up as a set up. You hit the down the line practice shots at the service line, short line, receiving line, halfway between the receiving line and the back wall and off the back wall. Hit at least 10 shots from each location trying for 100% accuracy. Proceed to practice the backhand using these same drills and using appropriate backhand mechanics previously discussed. The backhand will take much more practice to perfect than your forehand. *(Pictures 1 and 2)*

Picture 1

Picture 2

Picture 3

2. **Pinch Shot Drills:** To practice pinch shots, take a position in center court starting at the service line. Hit the ball after one bounce out in front of your front foot hitting a pinch shot to the right corner (use good pinch shot mechanics – especially make sure your feet are turned at a slight angle towards the right corner). Let the ball rebound off the corner, keeping the ball low and wait for it to rebound off the left corner wall. You then turn your body and feet at a slight angle toward the left and re-pinch the shot into the left corner. Hit 10 good pinch shots to each side then repeat these practice pinch shots from the short line, receiving line, halfway between the receiving line and the back wall and pinch both corners. Remember to make 10 good pinch shots from each location to both corners.
(Pictures 3)

Another pinch shot drill is to hit a high pinch shot off one corner that rebounds to the opposite front corner as a set-up for a pinch shot. You then set your body into proper position and re-pinch the shot. Again, hit at least 10 properly executed pinch shots to each corner before you quit this drill.

Picture 4

Picture 5

3. **Ceiling ball drills –** The drill to practice ceiling balls is to hit the down the line ceiling ball on your forehand, contacting the ball directly over your head and aiming the ball at the front ceiling lights. The ball then rebounds off the front wall, takes two bounces off the floor and without hitting the sidewall or bouncing off the back wall as a set-up. The ball should hug the sidewall as close as possible without touching the sidewall. Hit this shot continuously at least 10 times without a mistake before moving to the backhand ceiling shot. Complete this same drill using your backhand.
(Pictures 4 and 5)

Picture 6

A second drill is to hit cross-court ceiling balls, aiming for the front ceiling about three feet from the front wall and toward the center of the court. Bounce the ball off the front wall, angling it toward the back corner. Try to keep the ball off the sidewall and make it bounce twice on the floor before it hits the back wall.
(Pictures 6)

4. **Ceiling ball – Out of the air drill:** In this drill, you hit a ceiling ball that sets you up for a shot you can hit out of the air, practicing various shots such as pinches, kill shots, down the lines, and cross court passes. Start in the middle of the court, hit a ceiling shot that rebounds as a set-up, get back behind the ball with the legs set and racquet high and proceed to take the shot you wish to practice. You should use this drill to practice all forehand and backhand ceiling ball set-up shots.

5. **Set up drill off the front wall:** In this drill, you hit the ball off the front wall as a set-up and hit the shot you wish to practice out of the air or you can let the ball bounce once off the floor before you hit it. By hitting the ball off the front wall at various heights, you can vary your shots.

6. **Set-up drills off the back wall:** The first drill is to bounce the ball off the floor so that the ball then bounces off the back wall as a set-up. You then take the shot you wish to practice. In this drill, make sure you wait for the ball to hit in front of the front foot before taking your shot. The second drill requires you to set-up a back wall shot by first hitting the ball off the front wall high and hard, forcing it to hit the back wall on a fly and rebound as a set-up. Then take your appropriate shot.

Level 2: Practicing with a Partner

1. **Pinch Shot Drill (down the line set-up):** In this drill, Player X stands in center court and sets up the partner by hitting a down the line pass shot. Player O returns the shot with a forehand pinch shot. Use this drill to practice both forehand and backhand pinch shots.
(Picture 7)

2. **Pinch Shot Drill (cross court pass set-up):** Player O hits a cross court pass shot as a set-up to Player X, who then proceeds to return this shot with a properly executed pinch shot. Use this drill to practice both forehand and backhand pinch shots.
(Picture 8)

3. **Pinch and Re-pinch Shot Drill:** Player O hits a pinch shot to the right sidewall; it then rebounds off the front wall where Player X re-pinches into the left side wall. This pinch re-pinch drill is continued until one-person miss hits the ball. The ball is then picked up and the drill is restarted.
(Picture 9)

Picture 7

Picture 8

Picture 9

Picture 10

Picture 11

Picture 12

Picture 13

Picture 14

4. **Ceiling Shot- Down the Line Drill (wide angle pass set-up):** Player X hits a wide-angle pass to Player O who returns it with a ceiling shot or down the line pass shot. Once again use this drill to practice these shots to both forehand and backhand sides.
(Picture 10)

5. **Ceiling Ball Drills:**

   A. **Ceiling Ball Drill (Cross Court):** Player X hits a forehand cross-court ceiling shot to Player O who returns this shot by hitting a backhand cross-court ceiling shot. Continue to hit cross-court ceiling shots until someone makes a miss hit, then stop and repeat the process. The partners should switch places after hitting at least 10 properly executed ceiling shots.
   (Picture 11)

   B. **Forehand to Forehand – Ceiling Ball Drill:** Player X hits a forehand ceiling ball down the line shot to Player O, who returns it with a forehand ceiling ball down the line shot. Keep hitting these ceiling balls, rotating between each player until one player hits a bad shot, then stop and repeat the process until each player hits at least 10 good ceiling balls.
   (Picture 12)

   C. **Backhand to Backhand – Ceiling Ball Drill:** Player X hits a backhand ceiling ball down the line shot to player O who returns it with a backhand ceiling ball down the line shot. Keep hitting these ceiling balls, rotating between each player until one player hits a bad shot, then stop and repeat the process until each player hits 10 or more good ceiling balls.
   (Picture 13)

6. **Down the Line Drill (pinch shot set up):** With both players positioned at mid court, Player X hits a forehand pinch to the right side wall; it rebounds off the front wall where Player O hits a backhand down the line shot. After at least 10 properly executed down the line shots, this drill is then repeated to the backhand side.
(Picture 14)

7. Drive Serve Drills
   A. **Drive Serve With A Down The Line Return:** Player O practices the drive serve to the opponent's backhand or forehand and Player X returns the serve with a down the line pass shot.

   B. **Drive Serve With A Cross Court Return:** Player O hits a drive serve to Player X's forehand or backhand and Player X returns the serve with a crosscourt pass shot.

   C. **Drive Serve With A Ceiling Return:** Player O hits a drive serve to Player X's forehand or backhand and Player X returns the serve with a ceiling ball.

8. **Other Serve and Return of Serve Drills:** The same drills explained in the drive serve drills number 7 should be used with other serves such as the lob serve, Z serve, jam serve, etc. This would involve player O serving different serves (rather than the drive serve) to Player X, who will practice returning serves with down the lines, cross court passes and ceiling balls.

9. **Pinch, Down the Line Pass, Cross Court Pass Drills (set up off ceiling balls):** In these drills, player O sets up Player X (stationed at center court) with a ceiling shot. After the ball hits the ceiling, Player X runs to a position behind the ball, sets both feet with the racquet in a proper forehand position, steps into the ball out in front of the front foot and hits either a pinch shot, down the line pass, or cross court pass, depending on which shot you are practicing. Do these same drills to the backhand side.

10. **Cross Court Pass, Down the Line Pass and Pinch Drills (set up off the back wall):** These drills are set up when Player O hits a shot off the front wall that travels to the back wall and rebounds as a back wall set up to Player X. As the ball rebounds off the back wall, Player X follows it and then takes a position to hit the ball out in front of his front foot with either a cross court pass, pinch shot or down the line shot (depending on the shot you are practicing). In this drill, the set up shots should be hit as kill shots as low off the front wall as possible. Remember to hit these back wall set up shots to both the forehand and backhand sides.

Level 3- Practicing with a Partner, Applying Pressure

In Level 3, all the drills mentioned in Level 2 are executed the same way with one important difference. Player O (the set up man) now puts pressure on Player X (person practicing the shot) by retrieving the partner's practice shots. The point can then be played out.

CHAPTER 13

CHAPTER 14

TEAM PRACTICE OR CLASS INSTRUCTION

This chapter is primarily written for racquetball instructors or coaches, but may have some useful information toward any player wishing to improve their game.

Racquetball is a difficult sport to coach or teach with large groups as most students or players are at different levels of play. This makes it more difficult to design practices, as a beginner/D player cannot always perform the same drills (i.e. cut-off drills) that an Open/A player can. So how does a coach or instructor design a practice to accommodate these differences? Also, oftentimes we become so caught up working with beginner players as they need more work that not enough time is spent with the more advanced players. The reverse also happens in which we spend most of our time helping the best players, while the beginner players suffer. To assist with this dilemma, we have the following suggested guidelines in designing practices or classes for the two extreme groups:

1. At the first week of practice or class session, make everyone perform a pre-skills test that rates players on all major shots of the game. Included in this evaluation should be the basic skills necessary to compete beyond the beginner level. These skills include the proper execution of shots by dropping the ball and hitting them at a 50% or lower for beginner level play, 50%-69% rate for intermediate level players and a 70% or higher rate for advanced players. The shots include forehand and backhand, down the lines; cross-court passes, ceiling balls and pinch shots. They must also demonstrate proper execution of the following serves to both the forehand and backhand sides of the court: Drive serves; lob serves (high lob or half lob) and Z serves (low z or high z).

2. Players are then placed in one of these three categories: Beginner, intermediate, or advanced levels.

An example of a portion of the skills test for a forehand down the line follows:

Down the Line Skills Test for:

(Insert Players Name)					
	Forehand	Backhand		Forehand	Backhand
1. Short Line	10	10	out of 10	100%	100%
2. Receiving Line	10	9	out of 10	100%	90%
3. 3/4 Distance From Front Wall	7	6	out of 10	70%	60%
4. Off Back Wall	5	4	out of 10	50%	40%

An example of a drive serve skills test follows:

Drive Serve Skills Test for:

(Insert Players Name)					
	Forehand	Backhand		Forehand	Backhand
1. Center Court	8	7	out of 10	80%	70%
2. Left Side	9	8	out of 10	90%	80%
3. Right Side	7	7	out of 10	70%	70%

These skills tests should then be used to evaluate cross-court passes, ceiling balls, pinch shots, lob serves and z serves to both the forehand and backhand sides.

Once it is determined to which level the player belongs (beginning, intermediate or advanced), the drills and practices are designed accordingly. Also, whenever a player is placed in the beginner or intermediate group and feels he/she is able to execute the skills test shots that will advance him/her to the next level, they should be allowed to retake the test and advance to the next group if they pass.

Beginner Group Practices or Lessons

The drills used in this group should be designed around all the basic shots and serves that we mentioned in the skills test section. This group must work hard on refining their mechanics. Extra emphasis will be placed on backhand shots, as most beginners' backhands are weak. An example of a progression of practice drills for beginners follows:

Drill 1

Forehand mechanics are practiced with a ball, with the coach or instructor first demonstrating proper: v-grip, proper footwork, court position, swing and follow-through.

Drill 2

These same mechanics are then practiced while hitting the ball to the front wall without skipping it. Start players near the front wall, then slowly move them back to the receiving line, then, ³/₄ court, and finally off the back wall. Once the players can perform this drill, move the group to hitting the more specific shots of cross court passes (these drills are generally easier to hit than down the lines for beginners).

Drill 3

Each player hits 20 properly executed forehand cross-court passes from shallow court, then deep court before they are permitted to move to the next series of drills.

Drill 4

Forehand down the line shots are practiced from these four locations; service box, 5' line, ³/₄ court and back court – each player must hit 20 properly executed down the line shots from each position before moving on to the next set of drills.

Drill 5

Players must hit 20 properly executed ceiling shots from the forehand side. Emphasis is placed on keeping the ball from touching the sidewall or rebounding off the back wall.

Drill 6

Players are required to hit forehand pinch shots using proper forehand mechanics, but emphasizing turning the feet at an angle toward the sidewall they are hitting. Players must hit 20 forehand pinch shots from the short line. Then they must hit 20 properly executed pinch shots from the receiving line.

As you probably noticed, we first recommend that beginners practice their forehands, as these skills are generally much easier to learn than the skills of the backhand.

Backhand Drills

All of the six drills mentioned above for beginner forehand are repeated for the backhand. For example, drill 1 is repeated except the coach demonstrates proper backhand mechanics without the ball. In drill 2, the backhand is practiced with a ball from the same four spots mentioned in the forehand drill only on the backhand side.

The beginners next must master serves by learning to drill, drill, and drill!

Lob serves are easy to learn and should be practiced first.

Serve Drill 1

The high lob serve to the backhand side is demonstrated to the beginners. They then practice hitting the high lob trying to keep the ball off the back wall and barely touching the sidewall and landing it deep in the backcourt. Players need to hit 20 accurate high lob serves before they quit.

Serve Drill 2

The half lob serve is demonstrated by the instructor/coach. The players are to make sure that the ball lands past the short line, but before the receiving line and bounces twice before the back wall. Players must hit 20 good serves before moving to the next drill.

Serve Drill 3

The drive serve is practiced by hitting it to both the back corners with emphasis placed on hitting the right angle. With beginners, don't expect perfect serves! Slowly encourage them to hit these serves lower. Make sure they hit 20 serves to both sides of the court that hit at a minimum angle into the back corner. Don't be too concerned if they fail to hit the ball off the floor with two bounces or fail to hit it just beyond the short line as you might expect from more advanced players. They are still learning footwork, follow through, and other aspects of a good serve.

Serve Drill 4

Z serves are practiced after the instructor demonstrates the proper mechanics of the hard-low z serve, medium-height z serve and the high z serve. Hitting to both rear corners practices Z serves. With beginners, it is more important that they concentrate making the ball hit the front wall first, not the side wall, on their initial hit and to have the ball come off the opposite side wall after the ball hits the floor rather than the back wall as a set up. They can worry about hitting the ball with power and more accuracy later. When each player hits 20 of each serve using the criteria mentioned previously, he/she moves on to the next drill.

At the beginner level, we recommend serves being practiced from within the service box either from the center of the box or one step to either side of the center of this box. As players become for proficient at these spots, they can later experiment serving from other areas of the serving box.

Remember to be very patient with beginners, as it is often frustrating trying to hit accurate shots. After the first few days or as soon as the players can hit the ball to the front wall, teach them the rules of the game and allow them to play each other after each drill are practiced. This way they can see how easy and fun it is to play and they will not be bored. However, constantly reinforce the idea that to improve they must practice drills.

Intermediate Level Practices

The same drills should be used for the intermediate groups that were used with beginners at the start of practices or class sessions. However, intermediate level players should move through these drills much more quickly than beginners and the more advanced drills listed should then be used to increase intermediate level performances.

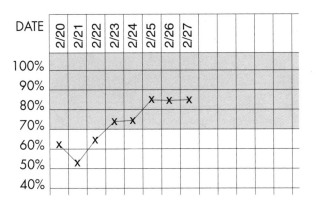

Advanced Level Drills

To become proficient at a top level, players should practice their shots by hitting the ball as it comes off the wall not just drop and hit. Players need to hit 3 sets of 10 of each shot and record their percentage so they can see their daily, weekly and monthly progress. Shots to be used are:

SHOTS

Down-The-Line Pass Shot	Forehand and Backhand
Ceiling Ball Shot	Forehand and Backhand
Cross Court V and Wide Angle Shot	Forehand and Backhand
Pinch Shot	Forehand and Backhand
Reverse Pinch Shot	Forehand and Backhand
Splat Shot	Forehand and Backhand
Kill Shot	Forehand and Backhand
Overhand Shot	Forehand and Backhand

SERVES

Drive Serves

Jam Serves

Lob Serves

Z Serves

Players should advance toward a success rate of 70% - 80% based on sets of 10 (3 sets) to become proficient at an advanced level. Practice with a partner if possible to induce some added pressure. After practicing, you should average the percentage of each set of 10 shots and place an x on the chart corresponding with the correct date. At the end of each week, you should then connect the x's to complete the graph. (shown lower left) This will show you your progress toward becoming a consistent racquetball player. Remember, you are only as good as the pressure that is exerted against you. Practice charts are shown on the next page. You can adapt these charts for every shot and serve. Remember to record your dates and percentages for all drills.

Forehand - Down the Line

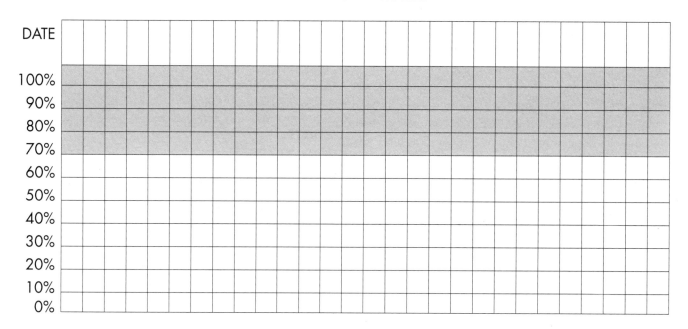

Backhand - Down the Line

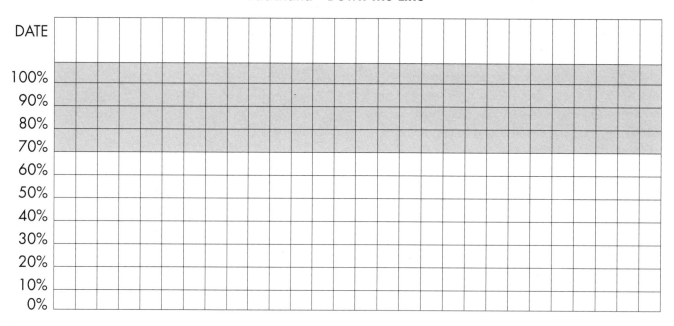

Alternative Workouts

On the court sprints and agility drills

These are an ideal way to practice improving quickness and conditioning. Do at least five sets of this drill after your games or practice sessions.

Drill 1: Line Touch Drill – Starting at the back wall of the court, sprint forward touching the front service box line with the right hand and sprint to the back wall. Continue the process by sprinting to the back service box line touching it with your left hand and sprint to the back wall. Finish by sprinting to the 5' line, touching it with your right hand and sprinting to the back wall.

Drill 2: Slide Step Drill –Starting at the back wall of the court with your entire body parallel to the side wall, use a shuffle step whereby your front foot slides sideways along the floor until your back foot makes contact with the front foot, then the front foot slides forward along the floor and the back foot once again slides forward until it touches the front foot. This procedure is repeated until the front foot reaches the front wall. The procedure is continued in the opposite direction until you've shuffle stepped all the way to the back wall four times down and back.

Drill 3: Star Drill – Use the slide step by beginning in the center of the court. Proceed to slide to one corner of the court and then return to the center and touch the floor. Continue this process by sliding to each corner and sidewall making a star pattern.

Star Drill

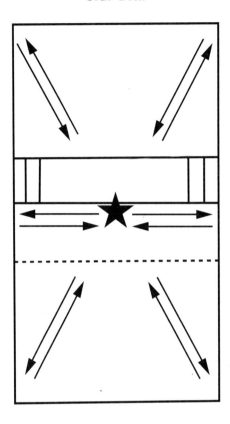

CHAPTER 15

HISTORY

Racquetball was first played and organized by a handball player named Joe Sobek in Greenwich, Connecticut, in 1949. He called the new game Paddle Racquets. The racquet was a strung paddle racquet and combined the rules of handball and squash. A man named Robert Kendler, who was the President of the U.S. Handball Association, popularized the game in the 50's.

In 1969, Paddle Racquets was renamed Racquetball and the International Racquetball Association (IRA) was formed. Ken Porco was named the IRA Executive Secretary.

Bruce Held and the Ektelon Company used the first metal racquet in 1970. Also in 1970, Robert Kendler was elected the President of the IRA. At this time, there were approximately 50,000 amateur players in the United States.

The first professional tour was formed in 1972. Chuck Lerie was also named IRA Executive Secretary. The fiberglass racquet frames were first used in competition in 1972.

In 1973, Robert Kendler left the IRA and formed the National Racquetball Club professional group. DeWitt Shy was named the IRA President and Myron Roderick was named the IRA Executive Director. This same year, the first established age groups were instituted in Juniors, Masters and Golden Masters.

In 1974, the IRA held the first professional tournament. There were approximately 3 million amateur racquetball players at this time. The next year, 1975, Tom McKie was named the IRA Executive Director.

The International Racquetball Association (IRA) saw a rival organization form in 1976. The new racquetball association was called the United States Racquetball Association (USRA). In the late 70's, racquetball became a fitness rage. In 1978, the IRA reorganized and was lead by Luke St. Onge who became its Executive Director. Bob Folson was named as the IRA president.

In 1979, the IRA changed its name to the American Amateur Racquetball Association (AARA).

The game of racquetball became organized on an international level when in 1979, 13 countries organized to found the International Amateur Racquetball Federation (IARF). In 1980, Keith Calkins became the board president and Han van der Hiejen of Holland became the IARF president.

The Women's Professional Racquetball Association (WPRA) was founded in 1980. Also in 1980, the form graphite racquet frame was introduced.

The first racquetball World Championship was held in Santa Clara, California in 1981. The USA won this world cup.

In 1984, the First National Elite Training Camp was held at the Olympic Training Center in Colorado Springs. This was one year after the AARA had relocated its headquarters to Colorado Springs. Match rules for racquetball changed in 1984 from 21 points to 15 points per game with an 11-point tiebreaker.

In 1985, the International Olympic Committee (IOC) recognized racquetball. The next year the mandatory eye guard's rule was instituted. Also in 1986, the Pan American Racquetball Confederation (PARC) was formed.

Racquetball was finally televised at the 1988 AARA National Championships. It was estimated that 10 million amateur players participated in racquetball during this time.

A significant event happened in the sport of racquetball in 1989 when the United States Olympic Committee (USOC) granted the sport full membership. That same year racquetball was added to the U. S. Olympic Festival held in Oklahoma City. Also in 1989, the first Senior/Masters Championships were held in Albuquerque, New Mexico.

Thirty-three countries competed in the 1992 World Cup in Montreal. This World Cup was won by the USA.

Racquetball made its debut in the Pan American Games in Buenos Aires, Argentina in 1995.

A premier racquetball event was established in Memphis, Tennessee in 1996. The Promos Hotel Corporation U.S. Open Racquetball Championships invited professional and amateurs to compete in this prestigious event. A glass court was built to maximize television coverage and enable hundreds of spectators to watch the matches.

The AARA changed its name to the United States Racquetball Association (USRA) in 1997. Oversized racquets with a maximum length of 22" were introduced this same year.

In 1998, the World Cup was held in Bolivia with 32 countries participating. Otto Dietrich was elected Board President of the USRA.

Jim Hiser was named Executive Director of the USRA in 2002 as Luke St. Onge resigned to accept a directorship of USOC and International Relations for the USRA.

This brief history was taken from 1998-1999 USRA racquetball fact book, published in the September/October issue of Racquetball™ Pages F2-F3. Permission granted by the United States Racquetball Association to publish this history.

The 2002 history brief was taken from Racquetball™ Page 32. Publication of the United States Racquetball Association, March/April 2002.

CHAPTER 16

BASIC RULES

1. The Game

a. **Types of Games** – When two play, it is called singles and when four play it is called doubles. A non-tournament game played by three players is called cutthroat.

b. **Points and Outs** – Points are scored only by the serving side. Losing the serve is called a side out in singles. In doubles, when the first server looses the serve, it is called a handout and when the second server, loses the serve it is a side out.

c. **Match, Game and Tiebreaker** – A match is won by the first side winning two games. The first two games of a match are played to 15 points. If each side wins one game, a tiebreaker game is played to 11 points.

2. Courts and Equipment

a. **Court Specifications** – The four-wall racquetball court is 20 feet wide, 40 feet long and 20 feet high with a back wall at least 12 feet high. Courts are marked with 1-$\frac{1}{2}$ inch wide lines (short line, service line, drive serve lines and receiving line) that indicate the service zone, service boxes and receiving zone.

b. **Racquet Specifications** – The racquet, including bumper guard and handle, may not exceed 21 inches in length. The frame may be any material judged to be safe, with a thong that securely attaches it to the player's wrist, and string that does not mark the ball.

c. **Apparel** – In sanctioned tournament play, eyewear designed for racquetball (which meets or exceeds ASTM F803 or Canadian [CSA] impact standards) is required. Players who require corrective eyewear also must adhere to this rule. Protective eyewear must be worn as designed and may not be altered. Shoes must not mark or damage the floor. Approved eyewear must be worn and wrist thongs must be used during warm-ups.

3. Play Regulations

a. **Serve** – The server has two opportunities to put the ball into play. In tournament play, the player or team winning the coin toss has the option to either serve or receive at the start of the first game. The second game will begin in reverse order of the first game. The player or team scoring the highest total of points in games one and two will have the option to serve or receive first at the start of the tiebreaker. In the event that both players and teams score an equal number of points in the first two games, another coin toss will take place and the winner of the toss will have the option to serve or receive. In everyday play, the lag or courtesy "you serve" will determine the first server.

b. **Start** – The serve is started from any place within the **service zone**; with the exception of certain drive serves. (See "Drive Serve Zones") Stepping on, but not over, the lines is permitted. The server may not step over the short line until the ball passes the short line.

c. **Manner** – The player begins the service motion with any continuous movement, which results in the ball being served. The ball must be bounced and hit before it bounces a second time.

d. **Drive Service Zones** – The drive serve lines are three feet from each sidewall in the service box. The player may drive serve between the body and the nearest side wall only if the player starts and remains outside of the 3-foot drive service zone and the racquet does not break the plane of the zone while making contact with the ball. The drive serve zones aren't observed for cross-court drive serves, the hard –Z, soft –Z, lob or half-lob serves.

e. Serve in doubles – At the beginning of each doubles game, when the first server is out, the team is out. Thereafter, both players on each team serve until the team receives a handout and a side out. On each serve, the server's partner must stand erect with their back to the sidewall and both feet on the floor within the service box until the served ball passes the short line.

f. Defective Serve – There are three types of defective serves: 1.) A dead ball serve which results in no penalty and the server is given another serve (like a wet spot or broken ball), 2.) Any fault serve (foot fault, short, long, screen, three-wall, etc.) and 3.) An out serve which results in an out. (double fault, server hits self with serve, etc.)

g. Return – Once a "good serve" puts the ball into play, the receiver may not enter the marked safety zone until the ball bounces or crosses the plane of the dashed receiving line – particularly in making an on-the-fly return attempt. After "legal" contact with the ball (after the bounce, or behind the line), the receiver's follow-through may carry the racquet or the body past the receiving line. Failure to return a serve results in a point for the server.

h. Side Out – A server continues to serve until an out serve, OR two consecutive faults serves, OR one player hits partner with an attempted return (in doubles), OR a player or team loses a rally, OR a player or team commits an avoidable hinder. In singles, retiring the server is a side out. In doubles, the side is retired when both partners have lost service.

i. Rally – Play initiated after the successful return of serve is called the rally. Play stops when: the ball is carried (resting on the racquet long enough that the effect is more of a sling or throw than a hit); the ball caroms off a players racquet into a gallery or wall opening; a ball obviously doesn't have the velocity or direction to hit the front wall and strikes another player; an avoidable hinder occurs. The ball remains in play until it touches the floor a second time, regardless of how many walls it makes contact with-including the front wall. In singles, if a player swings at the ball and misses it, the player may continue to attempt to return the ball until it touches the floor for the second time. In doubles, if one player swings at the ball and misses it, both partners may make further attempts to return the ball until it touches the floor the second time. Both partners on a side are entitled to return the ball.

j. Hinder – There are two types of hinders, 1) a dead-ball hinder, which is replayed without penalty (court hinders, body contact, safety holdup, screens, etc) and 2) avoidable, which result in the loss of rally by the offender (these are offensive shots from your opponent, like blocking, making distracting noise, or playing so close as to be hit by the backswing, etc.). If your court position or manner takes away an offensive shot from your opponent, the right thing to do is call an avoidable hinder on yourself.

Basic Self-Officiating

1. **Score** – Since there is not referee or scorekeeper, it is important for the server to announce both the server's and receiver's score before each first serve.

2. **During Rallies** – During rallies, it is the hitter's responsibility to make the call. If there is a possibility that a skip ball, double bounce or illegal hit occurred, play should continue until the hitter makes the call against their own shot. If the hitter does not make the call and goes on to win the rally, and the opponent thought that one of the hitter's shots was not good, they may appeal to the hitter by pointing out which shot was thought to be bad and request that the hitter reconsider. If the hitter is sure of the call, and the opponent is still sure the hitter is wrong, the rally should be replayed. As a matter of etiquette, players are expected to make calls against themselves any time they are not sure. Unless the hitter is certain the shot was good, it should be replayed.

3. **Service** –
   a. **Fault Serves** – The receiver has the primary responsibility to make these calls, though either player may make the call. The receiver must make the call immediately, and not wait until the ball has been hit to fain the benefit of seeing how good a return they have made; it is not an option play. The receiver does not have the right to play a short serve just because it could be a set-up.

   b. **Screen Serves** –When there is no referee, the screen serve call is the sole responsibility of the receiver. If the receiver has taken the proper court position, near center court, and he does not have clear view of the ball, the screen should be called immediately. Receivers may not call a screen after attempting to hit the ball or after taking themselves out of proper court position by starting the wrong way. The server may not call a screen under any circumstances and must expect to play the rally unless the receiver makes a call.

   c. **Other Situations** – Foot Faults, 10-second violations, receiving zone violations, and other calls may require a referee. However, if either player believes an opponent is abusing any of the rules, be sure there is agreement on what the rule is and have a clear understanding that the rules should be followed.

4. **Avoidable Hinders** – Since avoidable hinders are usually unintentional, they can occur even in the friendliest matches. A player who realizes that they have caused such a hinder should simply declare the opponent the winner of the rally. If a player feels that the opponent caused such a hinder, but the opponent does not make the call, the offended player should point out that an avoidable hinder occurred. However, unless the opponent agrees that an avoidable hinder occurred, it should not be called. Often just pointing out what appears to have been an avoidable hinder will prevent the opponent from such actions on future rallies.

5. **Disputes** – If either player, for any reason desires to have a referee, it is considered common courtesy for the other player to go along with the request, and a referee suitable to both sides should be found. If there is no referee, and a question about a rule or rule interpretation comes up, seek out the club pro or a more experienced player. Then, after the match, contact your state racquetball association for an interpretation.

The rules section was taken from the 2001 edition racquetball rule book, Official Rules of Racquetball-2001 Edition. Permission granted by the United States Racquetball Association. For detailed rules please contact the United States Racquetball Association, 1685 West Unitah, Colorado Springs, CO 80904-2906.

Real Racquetball Terms

Abdominals
Muscles located around the stomach area that bend and rotate the spine, twist and turn, support internal organs, and control the curvature of the spine and pelvic tilt.

Abductors
Muscles (gluteus medius and minimus) that move the legs out to the side and turn the hip outward.

Ace
Unreturned serve that earns a point.

Adductors
Muscles (inner thigh) that pull the legs and feet toward the body.

Aerobic
Activity such as jogging, bicycling, and walking whereby the amount of oxygen carried to the cells is adequate to maintain the activity.

Agility Drills
Exercise that increases the ability to move quicker and more fluently.

Alley
Imaginary target area along sidewalls for Down the Line shots.

Anti-Fog
A solution that is applied to eyewear that prevents residue buildup and allows the player to see clearly.

Amateur
A racquetball player that is not competing on the Professional Tour. Divisions include: Novice, D, C, B, A, Open and Age Categories.

Anaerobic
High intensity activity such as sprints or climbing stairs that causes the cells to be without oxygen (oxygen dept) that must be repaid later.

Around the World
A shot that hits side wall, front wall, and opposite side wall before touching the floor; also called "Around the Wall."

Backhand
Side of the body opposite the racquet hand. Also used to denote all shots initiated from that side of the body.

Back Rows
Weight training exercise that works the back muscles.

Ball
Standard ball has 2 1/4" diameter and weighs approximately 1.4 ounces. At a temperature of 70-74° F, a USRA approved ball will bounce 68" – 72" when dropped from a 100" height.

Bench Press
Weight training exercise that works the chest muscles (pectorals) and is performed on a flat or inclined bench.

Biceps
Muscles located on the upper front of the arms that flex the elbows.

Bye
A player advances through the first round of a tournament without having to play a match.

Ceiling Shot
Hits the ceiling before hitting the front wall (can also hit the front wall first as long as it immediately hits the ceiling next) and lands deep in the court.

Center Court
Area in the middle of the court, directly behind the short line.

Chest Fly
Weight training exercise that works the chest muscles and is performed with the lower back supported.

Coil
The body is placed in a ready-to-hit position.

Court
The standard racquetball court is 40' long, 20' wide, and 20' high, with a back wall at least 12' high. All surfaces are in play, with the exception of gallery openings and surfaces designated as court hinders prior to commencement of play. Court markings are 1 1/2" wide, red lines.

Cross Court (Pass)

A shot from one side of the court that hits the front wall and travels in a V or wide angle to the opposite rear corner. The purpose of the shot is to pass the opponent.

Crunches

A half sit-up whereby the shoulder blades are lifted to a 45-degree angle off the floor or off of a medicine ball and the lower back stays flat on the floor/medicine ball.

Curls

Weight training exercise that flexes the elbow and works the bicep muscles.

Cutthroat

A three-person, non-tournament variation of the game, with the server playing against the other two.

Dead Ball

Ball is no longer in play.

Defensive Shot

Any shot that prolongs, rather than ends, the rally. Typically move the opponent into deep court, i.e., a ceiling ball.

Deltoids

Shoulder muscles that cause the arms to lift and carry things.

Doubles

A game consisting of a two-person team playing another two-person team.

Down the Line

A shot hit near a sidewall that travels in a straight line to the front wall and straight back without hitting the sidewall.

Draw

The process of selecting tournament starting positions, or the actual draw sheets or brackets showing winners of each round.

Drive

A powerfully hit ball that travels in a straight line.

Drive Serve

A serve that is hit hard and low.

Drive Serve Lines

They form the Drive Serve Zone within the Serve Zone. A Drive Serve Line on each side of the court is parallel to, and three feet from, the sidewall. It is also called "Three-Foot Line."

Drive Service Zone

The area in the Service Zone between the sidewall and Drive Serve (Three Foot) Line. There is one on each side of the court.

Drop Shot

A shot that is hit softly to the front wall and drops to the floor.

Eye guards

Manufactured specifically for racquet sports and designed to protect the eyes. Eye guards are required for all USRA sanctioned play. Contact the USRA for a list of approved eyewear.

Fault

Illegal serve, such as: short, long, ceiling, three wall, out-of-court, screen, or missed. Or, infraction of rules while serving, such as, a foot fault. Two consecutive faults result in "side out." In one-serve divisions, one fault results in a side out.

Fitness

The measure of one's physical condition.

Five-Foot Line

Broken line 5' behind, and parallel to, the short line. It is also called the receiving line. It marks the boundary of the safety zone, which is in effect only during the serve and return of serve.

Flexibility

The ability of the muscles to move a body part (arm, leg, hand, foot) easily and with a wide range of movement.

Foot Fault

This occurs when the server's foot completely crosses over the service line during the serve or extends over the short line during the serve. In doubles, when the server's partner is not within the boundaries of the service box during the serve.

Forehand

The racquet side of the body. Also refers to all shots initiated from that side of the body.

Forehand Extensors

Muscles of the forearm that pull the hand back toward the forehand.

Forehand Flexors

Muscles of the forearm that bend the hand down.

Forfeit

Loss of a match by a player as a result of the player's "no-show" or other inability to play the scheduled match.

Front Court

Area from the service line to the front wall. (15')

Game

Played by two or four players. A two-person game is called singles and a four-person game is called doubles. Cutthroat is a non-tournament three-person variation. The objective of a game is to win each rally by serving or returning the ball in a way that prevents the opponent from keeping the ball in play. A rally is over when a player (or doubles team) cannot hit the ball before it bounces twice on the floor, or cannot return the ball so that it hits the front wall before it touches the floor. (A rally can be stopped and replayed without penalty if one player "hinders" another player's ability to see or hit the ball.)

Game Point

When the server is going for the point to win the game.

Gastrocnemius

One of two muscles of the calf that flex the foot downward.

Grip

The manner in which the racquet is held during play. Also refers to the material that covers the racquet handle.

Hamstrings

The muscles on the upper back part of the leg that enables the knee to bend and the hip to extend.

Heart Rate

The number of times your heart beats in one minute.

Hinder

Interference with a player's fair chance to make a shot. Includes a screen, which is to obstruct the receiver's view of the ball. If a hinder is called, the point is replayed without penalty.

Jam Serve

A hard drive serve that angles off the sidewall to hit at the receiver's feet.

Kill Shot

A racquetball shot that hits hard and low on the front wall that cannot be returned.

Latissimus Dorsi

Muscles that are located in the middle of the back that extend the arm, open the shoulder, rotate the arm inward and pull the shoulders down and back.

Lob Serve

Category of serves that rebound off the front wall in a high arc deep into the backcourt.

Long Serve

A fault serve that hits the back wall before hitting the floor.

Match

A complete racquetball competition won by the first person or team to win two games. The first two games of a match are played to 15 points. If needed, a tiebreaker is played to 11 points.

Match Point

When the server is going for the point that will win the match.

Mechanics

Technical aspects of the racquetball swing.

Medicine Ball

Ball that is weighted and is used to perform strength exercises.

Mental Imagery

The ability to mentally picture a racquetball scene in your head.

Mental Toughness

The ability of the mind to enable the body to perform at the optimal levels.

Mid-Court

Can refer to the area between the service line and the broken line and short line.

Military Press

Weight training exercise whereby weights (dumbbells, barbells or shoulder press machine) are lifted from the shoulder area to a position directly over the head with the arms completely extended.

Nick Lob

A soft serve that is hit high on the front wall then travels to the deep court grazing the sidewall then hits the floor and bounces at an angle toward the back wall.

Obliques

Muscles that bend and rotate the spine.

Offensive Shot

Shot intended to end the rally.

Out of Court Ball

Ball hit out of the playing area.

Out Serve

Loss of serve as a result of: serve that does not first hit the front wall; a touched serve; safety zone violation; 10-second violation; fake serve.

Overhead Shot

When the point of contact with the ball is higher than the player's shoulder.

Pass Shot

Cross court, down the line, or overhead drive hit out of the opponent's reach into the back court.

Pinch Shot

Offensive shot hit very low into the sidewall (near the front wall) and rebounds to the front wall.

Ply-metrics

Exercises that are used to increase power and speed movements.

Point

A point is scored only by the server (or serving team) by serving or returning the ball so that the opponent fails to keep the ball in play. A rally is over when a player (or opposing doubles team) cannot hit the ball before it bounces twice on the floor or cannot return the ball to hit the front wall before it touches the floor. The first two games of a match are played to 15 points. A tiebreaker, if needed, is played to 11 points. The score should be called aloud by the server prior to each serve in a non-tournament play. The score is called prior to every first serve by the referee in tournament play.

Pressure

The act of applying force to an opponent in order to influence them to make a poor shot.

Quadriceps

The four main muscles of the front thigh that extend the knee.

Racquet

The only means of hitting the ball in a racquetball game. Frame and string can be made of any material considered to be safe. The string should not mark the ball. From bumper guard at the top of the racquet, to the end of the handle, the length of all solid parts cannot exceed 21". A racquet must have a thong for secure attachment to the player's wrist.

Rally

Exchange of shots following the serve that ends in a point or side out for the server.

Ranking

Relative abilities of tournament competitors.

Receiver

Player waiting serve.

Receiving Line

Broken line 5' behind the short line. During the serve and return of serve, the receiver cannot break the plane of this 5' line with the racquet or body unless the ball first bounces inside this safety zone.

Recoil

The follow – through motion of the arm after contact is made with the ball.

Repetitions
The number of times you complete a weight training movement.

Reverse Pinch
Offensive shot hit very low into the sidewall (near the front wall) opposite the hitter's forehand side. The ball rebounds from sidewall to front wall. A right-handed player hits a reverse pinch into the left sidewall and vice-versa.

Role Models
Person(s) that has played a major influence on the way another person plays racquetball.

Roll Out
The result of a shot hit so low on the front wall that it rebounds straight out on the floor without bouncing.

Safety Hinder
The interruption of a rally to prevent injury. This happens when a player holds up a shot to prevent hitting the opponent with the racquet or ball.

Safety Zone
The area between the back of the short line and the broken receiving line. This is observed only during serve and return of serve.

Safety Zone Violation
When the receiver breaks the plane of the broken 5' receiving line with the racquet or body, unless the ball has first bounced inside this safety zone. In doubles, it is a violation for the server's partner to enter the safety zone before the served ball crosses the short line.

Screen
This is when the opponent obstructs the receiver's view of the ball on a serve or shot. On a serve, a screen is a fault. During a rally shot, the rally is replayed without penalty.

Serve
The action or shot that begins play for a point or side out.

Server
The player who puts the ball into play that results in a point or side out.

Service Box
An 18" box at each end of the service zone. In doubles, the server's partner must stay in one of the boxes until the served ball crosses the short line.

Service Line
The front line of the service zone that is 15' from and parallel to the front wall.

Service Return
The shot executed by the receiver of the serve.

Service Zone
The 5' x 20' area between the service line and short line, from sidewall to sidewall. The server must stay in this zone during the serve.

Set Up
This situation provides an easy scoring opportunity.

Shock Absorbers
A small piece of equipment (usually made of plastic or rubber) that attaches to a racquetball racquet to absorb some of the vibration or shock from the racquet.

Short Serve
A fault serve that does not entirely cross the short line before hitting the floor.

Short Line
The back line of the service zone, 20' from the front wall. The short line divides the court into halves. A legal serve rebounds off the front wall and over this line before hitting the floor.

Side Out
In doubles, refers to the loss of service to the opposing team. In singles, the loss of service to the opponent is usually called out.

Singles
A racquetball game consisting of one player opposing another player.

Skip Ball
Any shot that hits the floor before reaching the front wall.

Soleus
One of two calf muscles that are used to flex the foot downward.

Splat

An offensive shot executed close to the sidewall and hit very hard and low into the sidewall. The ball rebounds, hits the front wall with a "splat" sound, and kicks out at a sharp angle.

Squat

Weight training exercise used to strengthen the leg muscles in which a weight is held at shoulder level and the legs slowly lower the weight toward the floor until the legs are bent at a 90° angle to the floor.

Strategic Shot

A skillfully placed shot with a purpose.

Strength Training

Exercise used to increase strength.

Stretches

Exercises used to increase flexibility of joints and muscles.

Sweat Bands

A band worn on the head to collect sweat.

Technical Foul

A point is deducted from the score of the person receiving the foul.

Thong

The strap attached to the end of the racquet handle that must be wrapped around the wrist during play.

Three-Foot Line

The line in the service zone parallel to and 3' from each sidewall. During execution of any type of drive serve, the racquet or the player, including the follow through of the servers swing, cannot break the plane of this line.

Tiebreaker

An 11 point game to determine the winner of a match that is tied at one game each.

Time Out

Each player is allowed two 30-second time outs per 15-point game and one-30 second time out in an 11-point tiebreaker.

Tournament

An organized and formally structured system of competitive play.

Training Methods

Exercise routines and practice methods used to prepare racquetball players for competition.

Triceps

Muscles located in the back of the upper arms that extend the elbows.

USRA

United States Racquetball Association. Official governing body for rules. To purchase a complete copy of the official rules, contact the USRA at 1685 W Unitah, Colorado Springs, CO 80904. Or call 719-635-5396.

Upper Body

Muscles of the body from the waist up.

Wallpaper Serve

Hugs the side wall and is very difficult to return. Also called a wallpaper shot.

Z Balls/Z Serves

Category of shots and serves in which the path of the ball forms a Z.

Adopted in part from "The Language of Racquetball" and "Official Rules of Racquetball," Racquetball Magazine, Official Publication of the American Amateur Racquetball Association, March/April 1995 and Jul/August 1994, respectively.

OFFICIAL RULES & REGULATIONS

COMPETITION POLICIES & PROCEDURES

NOTE: Changes to rules and regulations in Sections 1 through 10 must adhere to published rule change procedures. Remaining policy sections may be altered by vote of the USRA Board of Directors.

ALSO ...

OFFICIAL RULES & REGULATIONS

1 — THE GAME

Rule 1.1 TYPES OF GAMES
Racquetball is played by two or four players. When played by two, it is called singles and when played by four, doubles. A non-tournament variation of the game that is played by three players is called cut-throat.

Rule 1.2 DESCRIPTION
Racquetball is a competitive game in which a strung racquet is used to serve and return the ball.

Rule 1.3 OBJECTIVE
The objective is to win each rally by serving or returning the ball so the opponent is unable to keep the ball in play. A rally is over when a player (or team in doubles) is unable to hit the ball before it touches the floor twice, is unable to return the ball in such a manner that it touches the front wall before it touches the floor, or when a hinder is called.

Rule 1.4 POINTS AND OUTS
Only the serving side scores points, when a serve is irretrievable (an ace) or when a rally is won. Losing the serve is called a sideout in singles. In doubles, when the first server loses the serve it is called a handout and when the second server loses the serve it is a sideout.

Rule 1.5 MATCH, GAME, TIEBREAKER
The first side winning two games wins a match. The first two games of a match are played to 15 points. If each side wins one game, a tiebreaker game is played to 11 points.

2 — COURTS AND EQUIPMENT

Rule 2.1 COURT SPECIFICATIONS
The specifications for the standard four-wall racquetball court are:

(a) Dimensions. The dimensions shall be 20 feet wide, 40 feet long and 20 feet high, with a back wall at least 12 feet high. All surfaces shall be in play, with the exception of any gallery opening, surfaces designated as out-of-play for a valid reason (such as being of a very different material or not in alignment with the backwall), and designated court hinders.

(b) Markings. Racquetball courts shall be marked with lines 1 1/2 inches wide as follows:

1. Short Line. The back edge of the short line is midway between, and is parallel with, the front and back walls.

2. Service Line. The front edge of the service line is parallel with, and five feet in front of, the back edge of the short line.

3. Service Zone. The service zone is the 5' x 20' area bounded by the bottom edges of the side walls and by the outer edges of the short line and the service line.

4. Service Boxes. The service boxes, used in doubles play, are located at each end of the service zone and are designated by lines parallel with the side walls [see 4.2(b)]. The edge of the line nearest to the center of the court shall be 18 inches from the nearest side wall.

5. Drive Serve Lines. The drive serve lines, which form the drive serve zone, are parallel with the side wall and are within the service zone. The edge of the line nearest to the center of the court shall be three feet from the nearest side wall.

6. Receiving Line. The receiving line is a broken line parallel to the short line. The back edge of the receiving line is five feet from the back edge of the short line. The receiving line begins with a line 21 inches long that extends from each side wall. These lines are connected by an alternate series of six-inch spaces and six-inch lines. This will result in a line composed of 17 six-inch spaces, 16 six-inch lines, and two 21-inch lines.

7. Safety Zone. The safety zone is the 5' x 20' area bounded by the bottom edges of the side walls and by the back edges of the short line and the receiving line. The zone is observed only during the serve. See Rules 3.10(i) and 3.11(a).

Rule 2.2 BALL SPECIFICATIONS
(a) The standard racquetball shall be 2 1/4 inches in diameter; weigh approximately 1.4 ounces; have a hardness of 55-60 inches durometer; and bounce 68-72 inches from a 100-inch drop at a temperature of 70-74 degrees Fahrenheit.

(b) Only a ball having the endorsement or approval of the USRA may be used in a USRA sanctioned tournament.

Rule 2.3 BALL SELECTION
(a) A ball shall be selected by the referee for use in each match. During the match the referee may, based on personal discretion or at the request of a player or team, replace the ball. Balls that are not round or which bounce erratically shall not be used.

(b) If possible, the referee and players should agree to an alternate ball, so that in the event of breakage, the second ball can be put into play immediately.

Rule 2.4 RACQUET SPECIFICATIONS
(a) The racquet, including bumper guard and all solid parts of the handle, may not exceed 22 inches in length.

(b) The racquet frame may be any material judged to be safe.

(c) The racquet frame must include a cord that must be securely attached to the player's wrist.

(d) The string of the racquet must be gut, monofilament, nylon, graphite, plastic, metal, or a combination thereof, and must not mark or deface the ball.

(e) Using an illegal racquet will result in forfeiture of the game in progress or, if discovered between games, forfeiture of the preceding game.

Rule 2.5 APPAREL
(a) All players must wear lensed eyewear that has been warranted by its manufacturer or distributor as 1.) designed for use in racquetball and 2.) meeting or exceeding either the full ASTM F803 standard or Canadian (CSA) impact standard. This rule applies to all persons, including those who wear corrective lenses. The eyewear must be unaltered and worn as designed at all times. A player who fails to wear proper eyewear will be assessed a technical foul and a timeout to obtain proper eyewear [see rule 3.17(a)(9)]. A second infraction in the same match will result in immediate forfeiture of the match.

Certifications & Compliance. The USRA maintains a reference list of eyewear so warranted by their manu-facturers, and provides that list to each sanctioned event (an eyewear list dated more than 90 days prior to the first day of the tournament will be deemed invalid for the purpose of determining compliance with this eyewear rule). In addition, the list is available online at the USRA.org website (indexed under "eyeguards"), and individual copies may be requested by calling the USRA National Office at 719/635-5396.

To be used in sanctioned competition, protective eyewear must:

* bear a permanent, physical stamp of the appropriate "ASTM-F803" citation on the frame itself, OR

* appear on the ASTM reference listing, OR

* bear the "Protective Eyewear Certification Council" [PECC] seal of approval for the ASTM standard, OR

* be certified in writing by the maker that it complies with the required ASTM standard (in this instance, the player must be able to provide written, adequate proof - on demand - at any sanctioned event, before such eyewear may be used).

(b) Clothing and Shoes. The clothing may be of any color; however, a player may be required to change wet, extremely loose fitting, or otherwise distracting garments. Insignias and writing on the clothing must be considered to be in good taste by the tournament director. Shoes must have soles which do not mark or damage the floor.

(c) Equipment Requirements During Warm-up. Proper eyeguards [see 2.5(a)] must be worn and wrist cords must be used during any on-court warm-up period. The referee should give a technical warning to any person who fails to comply and assess a technical foul if that player continues to not comply after receiving such a warning.

3 — PLAY REGULATIONS

Rule 3.1 SERVE
In Open Division competition, the server will have one opportunity to put the ball into play [see section 5.0, for complete, one-serve modifications]. In all other divisions, the server will have two opportunities to put the ball into play.

The player or team winning the coin toss has the option to either serve or receive at the start of the first game. The second game will begin in reverse order of the first game. The player or team scoring the highest total of points in games 1 and 2 will have the option to serve or receive first at the start of the tiebreaker. In the event that both players or teams score an equal number of points in the first two games, another coin toss will take place and the winner of the toss will have the option to serve or receive.

Rule 3.2 START
The server may not start the service motion until the referee has called the score or "second serve." The serve is started from any place within the service zone. (Certain drive serves are an exception. See Rule 3.6.) Neither the ball nor any part of either foot may extend beyond either line of the service zone when initiating the service motion. Stepping on, but not beyond, the lines is permitted. However, when completing the service motion, the server may step beyond the service (front) line provided that some part of both feet remain on or inside the line until the served ball passes the short line. The server may not step beyond the short line until the ball passes the short line. See Rule 3.9(a) and 3.10(i) for penalties for violations.

Rule 3.3 MANNER

After taking a set position inside the service zone, a player may begin the service motion—any continuous movement that results in the ball being served. Once the service motion begins, the ball must be bounced on the floor in the zone and be struck by the racquet before it bounces a second time. After being struck, the ball must hit the front wall first and on the rebound hit the floor beyond the back edge of the short line, either with or without touching one of the side walls.

Rule 3.4 READINESS

The service motion shall not begin until the referee has called the score or the second serve and the server has visually checked the receiver. The referee shall call the score as both server and receiver prepare to return to their respective positions, shortly after the previous rally has ended.

Rule 3.5 DELAYS

Except as noted in Rule 3.5 (b), the referee may call a technical foul for delays exceeding 10 seconds.

(a) The 10-second rule applies to the server and receiver simultaneously. Collectively, they are allowed up to 10 seconds after the score is called to serve or be ready to receive. It is the server's responsibility to look and be certain the receiver is ready. If a receiver is not ready, they must signal by raising the racquet above the head or completely turning the back to the server. (These are the only two acceptable signals.)

(b) Serving while the receiving player/team is signaling not ready is a fault serve.

(c) After the score is called, if the server looks at the receiver and the receiver is not signaling not ready, the server may then serve. If the receiver attempts to signal not ready after that point, the signal shall not be acknowledged and the serve becomes legal.

Rule 3.6 DRIVE SERVICE ZONES

The drive serve lines will be 3 feet from each side wall in the service zone. Viewed one at a time, the drive serve line divides the service area into a 3-foot and a 17-foot section that apply only to drive serves. The player may drive serve between the body and the side wall nearest to where the service motion began only if the player starts and remains outside of the 3-foot drive service zone. In the event that the service motion begins in one 3-foot drive service zone and continues into the other 3-foot drive serve zone, the player may not hit a drive serve at all.

(a) The drive serve zones are not observed for cross-court drive serves, the hard-Z, soft-Z, lob or half-lob serves.

(b) The racquet may not break the plane of the 17-foot zone while making contact with the ball.

(c) The drive serve line is not part of the 17-foot zone. Dropping the ball on the line or standing on the line while serving to the same side is an infraction.

Rule 3.7 DEFECTIVE SERVES

Defective serves are of three types resulting in penalties as follows:

(a) Dead-Ball Serve. A dead-ball serve results in no penalty and the server is given another serve (without canceling a prior fault serve).

(b) Fault Serve. Two fault serves result in an out (either a sideout or a handout).

(c) Out Serve. An out serve results in an out (either a sideout or a handout).

Rule 3.8 DEAD-BALL SERVES

Dead-ball serves do not cancel any previous fault serve. The following are dead-ball serves:

(a) Court Hinders. A serve that takes an irregular bounce because it hit a wet spot or an irregular surface on the court is a dead-ball serve. Also, any serve that hits any surface designated by local rules as an obstruction rather than being out-of-play.

(b) Broken Ball. If the ball is determined to have broken on the serve, a new ball shall be substituted and the serve shall be replayed, not canceling any prior fault serve.

Rule 3.9 FAULT SERVES

The following serves are faults and any two in succession result in an out:

(a) Foot Faults. A foot fault results when:

1. The server does not begin the service motion with both feet in the service zone.

2. The server steps completely over the service line (no part of the foot on or inside the service zone) before the served ball crosses the short line.

(b) Short Service. A short serve is any served ball that first hits the front wall and, on the rebound, hits the floor on or in front of the short line either with or without touching a sidewall.

(c) Three Wall Serve. A three-wall serve is any served ball that first hits the front wall and, on the rebound, strikes both side walls before touching the floor.

(d) Ceiling Serve. A ceiling serve is any served ball that first hits the front wall and then touches the ceiling (with or without touching a side wall).

(e) Long Serve. A long serve is a served ball that first hits the front wall and rebounds to the back wall before touching the floor (with or without touching a side wall).

(f) Bouncing Ball Outside Service Zone. Bouncing the ball outside the service zone as a part of the service motion is a fault serve.

(g) Illegal Drive Serve. A drive serve in which the player fails to observe the 17-foot drive service zone outlined in Rule 3.6.

(h) Screen Serve. A served ball that first hits the front wall and on the rebound passes so closely to the server, or server's partner in doubles, that it prevents the receiver from having a clear view of the ball. (The receiver is obligated to take up good court position, near center court, to obtain that view.)

(i) In open division play, if a serve is called a screen, the server will be allowed one more opportunity to hit a legal serve. Two consecutive screen serves results in an out.

(j) Serving before the Receiver is Ready. A serve is made while the receiver is not ready as described in Rule 3.5(b).

Rule 3.10 OUT SERVES
Any of the following results in an out:

(a) Two Consecutive Fault Serves [see Rule 3.9], or a single fault serve in open division play [see exceptions: 5.0].

(b) Missed Serve Attempt. Any attempt to strike the ball that results in a total miss or in the ball touching any part of the server's body. Also, allowing the ball to bounce more than once during the service motion.

(c) Touched Serve. Any served ball that on the rebound from the front wall touches the server or server's racquet before touching the floor, or any ball intentionally stopped or caught by the server or server's partner.

(d) Fake or Balk Serve. Any movement of the racquet toward the ball during the serve which is non-continuous and done for the purpose of deceiving the receiver. If a balk serve occurs, but the referee believes that no deceit was involved, the option of declaring "no serve" and having the serve replayed without penalty can be exercised.

(e) Illegal Hit. An illegal hit includes contacting the ball twice, carrying the ball, or hitting the ball with the handle of the racquet or part of the body or uniform.

(f) Non-Front Wall Serve. Any served ball that does not strike the front wall first.

(g) Crotch Serve. Any served ball that hits the crotch of the front wall and floor, front wall and side wall, or front wall and ceiling is an out serve (because it did not hit the front wall first). A serve into the crotch of the back wall and floor is a good serve and in play. A served ball that hits the crotch of the side wall and floor beyond the short line is in play.

(h) Out-of-Court Serve. An out-of-court serve is any served ball that first hits the front wall and, before striking the floor, either goes out of the court or hits a surface above the normal playing area of the court that has been declared as out-of-play for a valid reason [See Rule 2.1(a)].

(i) Safety Zone Violation. If the server, or doubles partner, enters into the safety zone before the served ball passes the short line, it shall result in the loss of serve.

Rule 3.11 RETURN OF SERVE
(a) Receiving Position

1. The receiver may not enter the safety zone until the ball bounces or crosses the receiving line.

2. In making an "on the fly" return attempt, the receiver may not strike the ball until the ball breaks the plane of the receiving line. However, the receiver's follow-through may carry the receiver or the racquet past the receiving line.

3. Neither the receiver nor the racquet may break the plane of the short line, except if the ball is struck after rebounding off the back wall.

4. Any violation by the receiver results in a point for the server.

(b) Defective Serve. A player on the receiving side may not intentionally catch or touch a served ball (such as an apparently long or short serve) until the referee has made a call or the ball has touched the floor for a second time. Violation results in a point.

(c) Legal Return. After a legal serve, a player receiving the serve must strike the ball on the fly or after the first bounce, and before the ball touches the floor the second time; and return the ball to the front wall, either directly or after touching one or both side walls, the back wall or the ceiling, or any combination of those surfaces. A returned ball must touch the front wall before touching the floor.

(d) Failure to Return. The failure to return a serve results in a point for the server.

(e) Other Provisions. Except as noted in this rule (3.11), the return of serve is subject to all provisions of Rules 3.13 through 3.15.

Rule 3.12 CHANGES OF SERVE
(a) Outs. A server is entitled to continue serving until one of the following occurs:

1. Out Serve. See Rule 3.10.

2. Two Consecutive Fault Serves [see Rule 3.9], or a single fault serve in open division play [see exceptions: 5.0].

3. Failure to Return Ball. Player or team fails to keep the ball in play as required by Rule 3.11 (c).

4. Avoidable Hinder. Player or team commits an avoidable hinder which results in an out. See Rule 3.15.

(b) Sideout. Retiring the server in singles is called a sideout.

(c) Effect of Sideout. When the server (or serving team) receives a sideout, the server becomes the receiver and the receiver becomes the server.

Rule 3.13 RALLIES
All of the play that occurs after the successful return of serve is called the rally. Play shall be conducted according to the following rules:

(a) Legal Hits. Only the head of the racquet may be used at any time to return the ball. The racquet may be held in one or both hands. Switching hands to hit a ball, touching the ball with any part of the body or uniform, or removing the wrist safety cord during a rally results in a loss of the rally.

(b) One Touch. The player or team trying to return the ball may touch or strike the ball only once or else the rally is lost. The ball may not be carried. (A carried ball is one that rests on the racquet long enough that the effect is more of a sling, or throw, than a hit.)

(c) Failure to Return. Any of the following constitutes a failure to make a legal return during a rally:

1. The ball bounces on the floor more than once before being hit.

2. The ball does not reach the front wall on the fly.

3. The ball is hit such that it goes into the gallery or

wall opening or else hits a surface above the normal playing area of the court that has been declared as out-of-play [See Rule 2.1(a)].

4. A ball, which obviously does not have the velocity or direction to hit the front wall, strikes another player.

5. A ball struck by one player on a team hits that player or that player's partner.

6. Committing an avoidable hinder. See Rule 3.15.

7. Switching hands during a rally.

8. Failure to use a racquet wrist safety cord.

9. Touching the ball with the body or uniform.

10. Carrying or slinging the ball with the racquet.

(d) Effect of Failure to Return. Violations of Rules 3.13 (a-c) result in a loss of rally. If the serving player or team loses the rally, it is an out. If the receiver loses the rally, it results in a point for the server.

(e) Return Attempts. The ball remains in play until it touches the floor a second time, regardless of how many walls it makes contact with — including the front wall. If a player swings at the ball and misses it, the player may continue to attempt to return the ball until it touches the floor for the second time.

(f) Broken Ball. If there is any suspicion that a ball has broken during a rally, play shall continue until the end of the rally. The referee or any player may request the ball be examined. If the referee decides the ball is broken the ball will be replaced and the rally replayed. The server resumes play at first serve. The only proper way to check for a broken ball is to squeeze it by hand. (Checking the ball by striking it with a racquet will not be considered a valid check and shall work to the disadvantage of the player or team which struck the ball after the rally.)

(g) Play Stoppage

1. If a foreign object enters the court, or any other outside interference occurs, the referee shall stop the play immediately and declare a dead-ball hinder.

2. If a player loses any apparel, equipment, or other article, the referee shall stop play immediately and declare an avoidable hinder or dead-ball hinder as described in Rule 3.15 (i).

(h) Replays. Whenever a rally is replayed for any reason, the server resumes play at first serve. A previous fault serve is not considered.

Rule 3.14 DEAD-BALL HINDERS

A rally is replayed without penalty and the server receives resumes play at first serve whenever a dead-ball hinder occurs. Also see Rule 3.15, which describes conditions under which a hinder might be declared avoidable, and result in loss of the rally.

(a) Situations

1. Court Hinders. The referee should stop play immediately whenever the ball hits any part of the court that was designated in advance as a court hinder (such as a vent grate). The referee should also stop play (i) when the ball takes an irregular bounce as a result of contacting a rough surface (such as court light or vent) or after striking a wet spot on the floor or wall and (ii) when, in the referee's opinion, the irregular bounce affected the rally.

2. Ball Hits Opponent. When an opponent is hit by a return shot in flight, it is a dead-ball hinder. If the opponent is struck by a ball that obviously did not have the velocity or direction to reach the front wall, it is not a hinder, and the player who hit the ball will lose the rally. A player who has been hit by the ball can stop play and make the call though the call must be made immediately and acknowledged by the referee. Note this interference may, under certain conditions, be declared an avoidable hinder. See Rule 3.15.

3. Body Contact. If body contact occurs which the referee believes was sufficient to stop the rally, either for the purpose of preventing injury by further contact or because the contact prevented a player from being able to make a reasonable return, the referee shall call a hinder. Incidental body contact in which the offensive player clearly will have the advantage should not be called a hinder, unless the offensive player obviously stops play. Contact with the racquet on the follow-through normally is not considered a hinder.

4. Screen Ball. Any ball rebounding from the front wall so close to the body of the defensive player that it prevents the offensive player from having a clear view of the ball. (The referee should be careful not to make the screen call so quickly that it takes away a good offensive opportunity.) A ball that passes between the legs of a player who has just returned the ball is not automatically a screen. It depends on whether the other player is impaired as a result. Generally, the call should work to the advantage of the offensive player.

5. Backswing Hinder. Any body or racquet contact, on the backswing, or on the way to, or just prior to, returning the ball, which impairs the hitter's ability to take a reasonable swing. The player attempting the return can make this call, though the call must be made immediately and is subject to the referee's approval. Note the interference may be considered an avoidable hinder. See Rule 3.15.

6. Safety Holdup. Any player about to execute a return who believes that striking the opponent with the ball or racquet is likely, may immediately stop play and request a dead-ball hinder. This call must be made immediately and is subject to acceptance and approval of the referee. (The referee will grant a dead-ball hinder if it is believed the holdup was reasonable and the player would have been able to return the shot. The referee may also call an avoidable hinder if warranted.)

7. Other Interference. Any other unintentional interference which prevents an opponent from having a fair chance to see or return the ball. Example: When a ball from another court enters the court during a rally or when a referee's call on an adjacent court obviously distracts a player.

(b) Effect of Hinders. The referee's call of hinder stops play and voids any situation which follows, such as the ball hitting the player. The only hinders that may be called by a player are described in rules (2), (5), and (6) above, and all of these are subject to the approval of the referee. A dead-ball hinder stops play and the rally is replayed. The server resumes play at first serve.

(c) Responsibility. While making an attempt to return the ball, a player is entitled to a fair chance to see and return the ball. It is the responsibility of the side that has just hit the ball to move so the receiving side may go straight to the ball and have an unobstructed view of and swing at the ball. However, the receiver is responsible for making a reasonable effort to move towards the ball and must have a reasonable chance to return the ball for any type of hinder to be called.

Rule 3.15 AVOIDABLE HINDERS

An avoidable hinder results in the loss of the rally. An avoidable hinder does not necessarily have to be an intentional act. Dead-ball hinders are described in Rule 3.14. Any of the following results in an avoidable hinder:

(a) Failure to Move. A player does not move sufficiently to allow an opponent a shot straight to the front wall as well as a cross-court shot which is a shot directly to the front wall at an angle that would cause the ball to rebound directly to the rear corner farthest from the player hitting the ball. Also when a player moves in such a direction that it prevents an opponent from taking either of these shots.

(b) Stroke Interference. This occurs when a player moves,

or fails to move, so that the opponent returning the ball does not have a free, unimpeded swing. This includes unintentionally moving in a direction that prevents the opponent from making an open, offensive shot.

(c) Blocking. Moves into a position which blocks the opponent from getting to, or returning, the ball; or in doubles, a player moves in front of an opponent as the player's partner is returning the ball.

(d) Moving into the Ball. Moves in the way and is struck by the ball just played by the opponent.

(e) Pushing. Deliberately pushes or shoves opponent during a rally.

(f) Intentional Distractions. Deliberate shouting, stamping of feet, waving of racquet, or any other manner of disrupting one's opponent.

(g) View Obstruction. A player moves across an opponent's line of vision just before the opponent strikes the ball.

(h) Wetting the Ball. The players, particularly the server, should ensure that the ball is dry prior to the serve. Any wet ball that is not corrected prior to the serve shall result in an avoidable hinder against the server.

(i) Apparel or Equipment Loss. If a player loses any apparel, equipment, or other article, play shall be immediately stopped and that player shall be called for an avoidable hinder, unless the player has just hit a shot that could not be retrieved. If the loss of equipment is caused by a player's opponent, then a dead-ball hinder should be called. If the opponent's action is judged to have been avoidable, then the opponent should be called for an avoidable hinder.

Rule 3.16 TIMEOUTS
(a) Rest Periods. Each player or team is entitled to three 30-second timeouts in games to 15 and two 30-second timeouts in games to 11. Timeouts may not be called, by either side, after service motion has begun. Calling for a timeout when none remain or after service motion has begun, or taking more than 30 seconds in a timeout, will result in the assessment of a technical foul for delay of game.

(b) Injury. If a player is injured during the course of a match as a result of contact, such as with the ball, racquet, wall or floor, an injury timeout will be awarded. While a player may call more than one timeout for the same injury or for additional injuries that occur during the match, a player is not allowed more than a total of 15 minutes of rest for injury during the entire match. If the injured player is not able to resume play after total rest of 15 minutes, the match shall be awarded to the opponent.

1. Should any external bleeding occur, the referee must halt play as soon as the rally is over, charge an injury timeout to the person who is bleeding, and not allow the match to continue until the bleeding has stopped.

2. Muscle cramps and pulls, fatigue, and other ailments that are not caused by direct contact on the court will not be considered an injury. Injury time is also not allowed for pre-existing conditions.

(c) Equipment Timeouts. Players are expected to keep all clothing and equipment in good, playable condition and are expected to use regular timeouts and time between games for adjustment and replacement of equipment. If a player or team is out of timeouts and the referee determines that an equipment change or adjustment is necessary for fair and safe continuation of the match, the referee may grant an equipment timeout not to exceed 2 minutes. The referee may allow additional time under unusual circumstances.

(d) Between Games. The rest period between the first two games of a match is 2 minutes. If a tiebreaker is necessary, the rest period between the second and third game is 5 minutes.

(e) Postponed Games. Any games postponed by referees shall be resumed with the same score as when postponed.

Rule 3.17 TECHNICAL FOULS AND WARNINGS
(a) Technical Fouls. The referee is empowered to deduct one point from a player's or team's score when, in the referee's sole judgment, the player is being overtly and deliberately abusive. If the player or team against whom the technical foul was assessed does not resume play immediately, the referee is empowered to forfeit the match in favor of the opponent. Some examples of actions that can result in technical fouls are:

1. Profanity.

2. Excessive arguing.

3. Threat of any nature to opponent or referee.

4. Excessive or hard striking of the ball between rallies.

5. Slamming of the racquet against walls or floor, slamming the door, or any action that might result in damage to the court or injury to other players.

6. Delay of game. Examples include (i) taking too much time to dry the court, (ii) excessive questioning of the

referee about the rules, (iii) exceeding the time allotted for timeouts or between games, (iv) calling a timeout when none remain, or after the service motion begins, or (v) taking more than ten seconds to serve or be ready to receive serve.

7. Intentional front line foot fault to negate a bad lob serve.

8. Anything the referee considers to be unsportsmanlike behavior.

9. Failure to wear lensed eyewear designed for racquet sports [See Rule 2.5(a)] is an automatic technical foul on the first infraction, plus a mandatory timeout (to acquire the proper eyewear) will be charged against the offending player. A second infraction by that player during the match will result in automatic forfeiture of the match.

(b) Technical Warnings. If a player's behavior is not so severe as to warrant a technical foul, a technical warning may be issued without the deduction of a point.

(c) Effect of Technical Foul or Warning. If a referee issues a technical foul, one point shall be removed from the offender's score. No point will be deducted if a referee issues a technical warning. In either case, a technical foul or warning should be accompanied by a brief explanation. Issuing a technical foul or warning has no effect on who will be serving when play resumes. If a technical foul occurs when the offender has no points or between games, the result will be that the offender's score becomes minus one (-1).

RULE MODIFICATIONS

The following sections (4.0 through 11.0) detail the additional or modified rules that apply to variations of the singles game described in Sections 1 through 3.

4.0 — DOUBLES

The USRA's rules for singles also apply in doubles with the following additions and modifications:

Rule 4.1 DOUBLES TEAM
(a) A doubles team shall consist of two players who meet either the age requirements or player classification requirements to participate in a particular division of play. A team with different skill levels must play in the division of the player with the higher level of ability. When playing in an adult age division, the team must play in the division of the younger player. When playing in a junior age division, the team must play in the division of the older player.

(b) A change in playing partners may be made so long as the first match of the posted team has not begun. For this purpose only, the match will be considered started once the teams have been called to the court. The team must notify the tournament director of the change prior to the beginning of the match.

Rule 4.2 SERVE IN DOUBLES
(a) Order of Serve. Before the match begins, each team shall inform the referee of their team's order of service, which shall be followed throughout the match. The order of serve may be changed between games, provided that the referee has been verbally notified before the first serve of the new game. At the beginning of each game, when the first server of the first team to serve is out, the team is out. Thereafter, both players on each team shall serve until the team receives a handout and a sideout.

(b) Partner's Position. On each serve, the server's partner shall stand erect with back to the side wall and with both feet on the floor within the service box from the moment the server begins the service motion until the served ball passes the short line. Violations are called foot faults. However, if the server's partner enters the safety zone before the ball passes the short line, the server loses service.

(c) Changes of Serve. In doubles, the side is retired when both partners have lost service, except that the team, which serves first at the beginning of each game, loses the serve when the first server is retired.

Rule 4.3 FAULT SERVE IN DOUBLES
(a) The server's partner is not in the service box with both feet on the floor and back to the sidewall from the time the server begins the service motion until the ball passes the short line.

(b) A served ball that hits the doubles partner while in the doubles box results in a fault serve.

(c) In open division play, if a serve hits the non-serving partner while standing in the box, the server will be allowed one more opportunity to hit a legal serve. Hitting the non-serving partner twice results in an out.

(d) In open division play, consecutive faults — either (i) a screen serve followed by hitting the non-serving partner or (ii) hitting the non-serving partner followed by a screen serve — results in an out.

Rule 4.4 OUT SERVE IN DOUBLES
(a) Out-of-Order Serve. In doubles, when either partner serves out of order, the points scored by that server will be subtracted and an out serve will be called: if the second server serves out of order, the out serve will be

applied to the first server and the second server will resume serving. If the player designated as the first server serves out of order, a sideout will be called. The referee should call "no serve" as soon as an out-of-order serve occurs. If no points are scored while the team is out of order, only the out penalty will have to be assessed. However, if points are scored before the out of order condition is noticed and the referee cannot recall the number, the referee may enlist the aid of the line judges (but not the crowd) to recall the number of points to be deducted.

(b) Ball Hits Partner. A served ball that hits the doubles partner while outside the doubles box results in loss of serve.

Rule 4.5 RETURN IN DOUBLES

(a) The rally is lost if one player hits that same player's partner with an attempted return.

(b) If one player swings at the ball and misses it, both partners may make further attempts to return the ball until it touches the floor the second time. Both partners on a side are entitled to return the ball.

5.0 — ONE SERVE

The USRA's standard rules governing racquetball play will be followed, but only one serve is allowed. Therefore, any fault serve is an out serve, with a few exceptions [noted separately below, and within the text rules cited].

See Rule 3.9 FAULT SERVES
[Screens]

(i) In open division play, if a serve is called a screen, the server will be allowed one more opportunity to hit a legal serve. Two consecutive screen serves results in an out.

See Rule 4.3 FAULT SERVES IN DOUBLES
[Serve hits partner]

(c) In open division play, if a serve hits the non-serving partner while standing in the box, the server will be allowed one more opportunity to hit a legal serve. Hitting the non-serving partner twice, results in an out.

[Consecutive faults]

(d) In open division play, consecutive faults — either (i) a screen serve followed by hitting the non-serving partner or (ii) hitting the non-serving partner followed by a screen serve — results in an out

6.0 — MULTI-BOUNCE

In general, the USRA's standard rules governing racquetball play will be followed except for the modifications that follow.

Rule 6.1 BASIC RETURN RULE

In general, the ball remains in play as long as it is bouncing. However, the player may swing only once at the ball and the ball is considered dead at the point it stops bouncing and begins to roll. Also, anytime the ball rebounds off the back wall, it must be struck before it crosses the short line on the way to the front wall, except as explained in Rule 6.2.

Rule 6.2 BLAST RULE

If the ball caroms from the front wall to the back wall on the fly, the player may hit the ball from any place on the court—including past the short line—so long as the ball is still bouncing.

Rule 6.3 FRONT WALL LINES

Two parallel lines (tape may be used) should be placed across the front wall such that the bottom edge of one line is 3 feet above the floor and the bottom edge of the other line is 1 foot above the floor. During the rally, any ball that hits the front wall (i) below the 3-foot line and (ii) either on or above the 1-foot line must be returned before it bounces a third time. However, if the ball hits below the 1-foot line, it must be returned before it bounces twice. If the ball hits on or above the 3-foot line, the ball must be returned as described in the basic return rule.

Rule 6.4 GAMES AND MATCHES

All games are played to 11 points and the first side to win two games, wins the match.

7.0 — ONE-WALL & THREE-WALL PLAY

In general, the USRA's standard rules governing racquetball play will be followed except for the modifications that follow.

Rule 7.1 ONE-WALL

There are two playing surfaces—the front wall and the floor. The wall is 20 feet wide and 16 feet high. The floor is 20 feet wide and 34 feet to the back edge of the long line. To permit movement by players, there should be a minimum of three feet (six feet is recommended) beyond the long line and six feet outside each side line.

(a) Short Line. The back edge of the short line is 16 feet from the wall.

(b) Service Markers. Lines at least six inches long which are parallel with, and midway between, the long and short lines. The extension of the service markers form the imaginary boundary of the service line.

(c) Service Zone. The entire floor area inside and including the short line, side lines and service line.

(d) Receiving Zone. The entire floor area in back of the short line, including the side lines and the long line.

Rule 7.2 THREE-WALL WITH SHORT SIDE WALL

The front wall is 20 feet wide and 20 feet high. The sidewalls are 20 feet long and 20 feet high, with the side walls tapering to 12 feet high. The floor length and court markings are the same as a four wall court.

Rule 7.3 THREE-WALL WITH LONG SIDE WALL

The court is 20 feet wide, 20 feet high and 40 feet long. The sidewalls may taper from 20 feet high at the front wall down to 12 feet high at the end of the court. All court markings are the same as a four wall court.

Rule 7.4 SERVICE IN THREE-WALL COURTS

A serve that goes beyond the side walls on the fly is an out. A serve that goes beyond the long line on a fly, but within the side walls, is a fault.

8.0 — WHEELCHAIR

Rule 8.1 CHANGES TO STANDARD RULES

In general, the USRA's standard rules governing racquetball play will be followed, except for the modifications that follow.

(a) Where USRA rules refer to server, person, body, or other similar variations, for wheelchair play such reference shall include all parts of the wheelchair in addition to the person sitting on it.

(b) Where the rules refer to feet, standing or other similar descriptions, for wheelchair play it means only where the rear wheels actually touch the floor.

(c) Where the rules mention body contact, for wheelchair play it shall mean any part of the wheelchair in addition to the player.

(d) Where the rules refer to double bounce or after the first bounce, it shall mean three bounces. All variations of the same phrases shall be revised accordingly.

Rule 8.2 DIVISIONS

(a) Novice Division. The novice division is for the beginning player who is just learning to play.

(b) Intermediate Division. The Intermediate Division is for the player who has played tournaments before and has a skill level to be competitive in the division.

(c) Open Division. The Open Division is the highest level of play and is for the advanced player.

(d) Multi-Bounce Division. The Multi-Bounce Division is for the individuals (men or women) whose mobility is such that wheelchair racquetball would be impossible if not for the Multi-Bounce Division.

(e) Junior Division. The junior divisions are for players who are under the age of 19. The tournament director will determine if the divisions will be played as two bounce or multi-bounce. Age divisions are: 8-11, 12-15, and 16-18.

Rule 8.3 RULES

(a) Two Bounce Rule. Two bounces are used in wheelchair racquetball in all divisions except the Multi-Bounce Division. The ball may hit the floor twice before being returned.

(b) Out-of-Chair Rule. The player can neither intentionally jump out of the chair to hit a ball nor stand up in the chair to serve the ball. If the referee determines that the chair was left intentionally it will result in loss of the rally for the offender. If a player unintentionally leaves the chair, no penalty will be assessed. Repeat offenders will be warned by the referee.

(c) Equipment Standards. To protect playing surfaces, the tournament officials will not allow a person to participate with black tires or anything that will mark or damage the court.

(d) Start. The serve may be started from any place within the service zone. Although the front casters may extend beyond the lines of the service zone, at no time shall the rear wheels cross either the service or short line before the served ball crosses the short line. Penalties for violation are the same as those for the standard game.

(e) Maintenance Delay. A maintenance delay is a delay in the progress of a match due to a malfunction of a wheelchair, prosthesis, or assistive device. Such delay must be requested by the player, granted by the referee during the match, and shall not exceed 5 minutes. Only two such delays may be granted for each player for each match. After using both maintenance delays, the player has the following options: (i) continue play with the defective equipment, (ii) immediately substitute replacement equipment, or (iii) postpone the game, with the approval of the referee and opponent.

Rule 8.4 MULTI-BOUNCE RULES

(a) The ball may bounce as many times as the receiver wants though the player may swing only once to return the ball to the front wall.

(b) The ball must be hit before it crosses the short line on its way back to the front wall.

(c) The receiver cannot cross the short line after the ball contacts the back wall.

9.0 — VISUALLY IMPAIRED

In general, the USRA's standard rules governing racquetball play will be followed except for the modifications that follow.

Rule 9.1 ELIGIBILITY

A player's visual acuity must not be better than 20/200 with the best practical eye correction or else the player's field of vision must not be better than 20 degrees. The three classifications of blindness are B1 (totally blind to light perception), B2 (able to see hand movement up to 20/600 corrected), and B3 (from 20/600 to 20/200 corrected).

Rule 9.2 RETURN OF SERVE AND RALLIES

On the return of serve and on every return thereafter, the player may make multiple attempts to strike the ball until (i) the ball has been touched, (ii) the ball has stopped bouncing, or (iii) the ball has passed the short line after touching the back wall. The only exception is described in Rule 9.3.

Rule 9.3 BLAST RULE

If the ball (other than on the serve) caroms from the front wall to the back wall on the fly, the player may retrieve the ball from any place on the court—including in front of the short line — so long as the ball has not been touched and is still bouncing.

Rule 9.4 HINDERS

A dead-ball hinder will result in the rally being replayed without penalty unless the hinder was intentional. If a hinder is clearly intentional, an avoidable hinder should be called and the rally awarded to the non-offending player or team.

10.0 — DEAF

In general, the USRA's standard rules governing racquetball play will be followed except for the modifications which follow.

Rule 10.1 ELIGIBILITY

An athlete shall have a hearing loss of 55 db or more in the better ear to be eligible for any tournament for deaf athletes.

11.0 - MEN'S PROFESSIONAL [International Racquetball Tour/IRT]

In general, competition on the International Racquetball Tour [IRT] will follow the standard rules governing racquetball established by the USRA, except for the modifications that follow. Modifications for both professional tours are consistent, with one exception as noted in Rule 11.4.

Rule 11.1 GAME, MATCH

All games are played to 11 points, and are won by the player who scores to that level, with a 2-point lead. If necessary, the game will continue beyond 11 points, until such time as one player has a 2-point lead. Matches are played the best three out of a possible five games to 11.

Rule 11.2 APPEALS

The referee's call is final. There are no line judges, and no appeals may be made.

Rule 11.3 SERVE

Players are allowed only one serve to put the ball into play.

Rule 11.4 SCREEN SERVE

In IRT matches, screen serves are replayed

Rule 11.5 COURT HINDERS

No court hinders are allowed or called.

Rule 11.6 OUT-OF-COURT BALL

Any ball leaving the court results in a loss of rally.

Rule 11.7 BALL

All matches are played with the Penn Pro ball. The first, third, and fifth (if necessary) games of the match are started with a new ball.

Rule 11.8 TIMEOUTS

(a) Per Game. Each player is entitled to one 1-minute timeout per game.

(b) Between Points. The player has 15 seconds from the end of the previous rally to put the ball in play.

(c) Between Games. The rest period between all games is 2 minutes, including a fifth game tiebreaker.

(d) Equipment Timeouts. A player does not have to use regular timeouts to correct or adjust equipment, provided that the need for the change or adjustment is acknowledged by the referee as being necessary for fair and safe continuation of the match.

(e) Injury Timeout. Consists of two seven and one-half minute (7-1/2) timeouts within a match. Once an injury timeout is taken, the full seven and a half minutes (7-1/2) must be used, or it is forfeited.

12.0 - WOMEN'S PROFESSIONAL [Ladies Professional Racquetball Association/LPRA]

In general, competition in the Ladies Professional Racquetball Association [LPRA] will follow the standard rules governing racquetball established by the USRA, except for the modifications that follow.

Rule 12.1 SERVE, GAME, MATCH

Players are allowed only one serve to put the ball into play. All games are played to 11 points, and are won by the player who holds a two-point lead. Matches are played the best three out of a possible five games to 11.

COMPETITION POLICIES AND PROCEDURES

Sections A through D which follow contain mostly policies and procedures concerning competition, rather than "rules of play" which are subject to the formal rule change procedures. However, some of the topics that follow are still subject to the formal rule change procedures. In the next edition of the rulebook, they will be highlighted for ease of location.

A — TOURNAMENTS

A.1 DRAWS

(a) If possible, all draws shall be made at least two (2) days before the tournament commences. The seeding method of drawing shall be approved by the USRA.

(b) At USRA National events, the draw and seeding committee is comprised of the USRA's Executive Director, National Tournament Director, and the host tournament director. No other persons shall participate in the draw or seeding unless at the invitation of the draw and seeding committee.

(c) In local and regional tournaments the draw shall be the responsibility of the tournament director.

A.2 CONSOLATION MATCHES

(a) Each entrant shall be entitled to participate in a minimum of two matches. Therefore, losers of their first match shall have the opportunity to compete in a consolation bracket of their own division. In draws of less than seven players, a round robin may be offered. See A.6 about how to determine the winner of a round robin event.

(b) Consolation matches may be waived at the discretion of the tournament director, but this waiver must be in writing on the tournament application.

(c) Preliminary consolation matches will be two of three games to 11 points. Semifinal and final matches will follow the regular scoring format.

A.3 SCHEDULING

(a) Preliminary Matches. If contestants are entered in more than one division, it is likely that they will be required to play several times on the same day with little rest between matches. This is a risk assumed on entering multiple categories of play. If possible, schedules should provide at least one (1) hour of rest between matches.

(b) Final Matches. Where the possibility exists of one or more players reaching the finals in multiple divisions, it is recommended that these matches be scheduled several hours apart to assure more rest between the final matches. If this is not possible, it is recommended that a singles final be scheduled before any doubles final, and that at least one (1) hour of rest be allowed between matches.

(c) Conflicts. If a player reaches the finals of two divisions that are scheduled within the same hour, that player should be given the option of choosing which final is to be played first.

A.4 NOTICE OF MATCHES

After the first round of matches, it is the responsibility of each player to check the posted schedules to determine the time and place of each subsequent match. If any change is made in the schedule after posting, it shall be the duty of the tournament director to notify the players of the change.

A.5 FINISHES

Finalists must play off for first and second place, or determine a winner by some mutually acceptable method. Semi-finalists are not required to play off for third place. However, if one semifinalist wishes to play off and the other does not, the one willing to play shall be awarded third place. If no playoff for third place occurs, both semi-finalists will receive fourth place points.

A.6 ROUND ROBIN SCORING

The final positions of players or teams in round robin competition is determined by the following sequence:

a. Winner of the most matches;

b. In a two way tie, winner of the head-to-head match;

c. In a tie of three or more, the player who lost the fewest games is awarded the highest position.

1. If a two way tie remains, the winner of the head-to-head match is awarded the higher position.

2. If a multiple tie remains, the total "points scored against" each player in all matches will be tabulated and the player who had the least "points scored against" them is awarded the highest position. Note: Forfeits will count as a match won in two games. In cases where "points scored against" is the tiebreaker, the points scored by the forfeiting team will be discounted from consideration of "points scored against" all teams.

A.7 COURT ASSIGNMENTS
In all USRA sanctioned tournaments, the tournament director and/or USRA official in attendance may decide on a change of court after the completion of any tournament game, if such a change will accommodate better spectator conditions.

A.8 TOURNAMENT CONDUCT
In all USRA sanctioned tournaments, the referee is empowered to forfeit a match, if the conduct of a player or team is considered detrimental to the tournament and the game. See B.5(d) and (e).

A.9 SPECTATOR CONDUCT
In the event of disruptive or threatening behavior on the part of any spectator, relative, parent, guardian or coach at any USRA sanctioned event, the referee is empowered to address a "first offense" by enforcing sanction #1 detailed below. For additional infractions, the tournament director or USRA official in attendance, either of their own accord or at the request of the referee, is empowered to enforce sanctions #2 and #3 as warranted.

1. For the first offense: violator may watch, but not speak, while the athlete's match is being played.

2. For the second offense: violator may not watch the athlete's match, but may remain within the building.

3. For the third offense: violator will be removed from the club for the duration of the tournament, and pertinent authorities advised of the restriction. If a given situation so warrants, the tournament director or USRA official may invoke this sanction immediately and without previous offenses - in the interest of safety.

B — OFFICIATING

B.1 TOURNAMENT MANAGEMENT
A tournament director, who shall designate the officials, shall manage all USRA sanctioned tournaments.

B.2 RULES COMMITTEE
The tournament director should appoint a tournament rules committee to resolve any disputes that the referee, tournament desk, or tournament director cannot resolve. The committee, composed of an odd number of persons, may include state or national officials, or other qualified individuals in attendance who are prepared to meet on short notice. The tournament director should not be a member of this committee.

B.3 REFEREE APPOINTMENT AND REMOVAL
The principal official for every match shall be the referee who has been designated by the tournament director, or a designated representative, and who has been agreed upon by all participants in the match. The referee's authority regarding a match begins once the players are called to the court. The referee may be removed from a match upon the agreement of all participants (teams in doubles) or at the discretion of the tournament director or the designated representative. In the event that a referee's removal is requested by one player or team and not agreed to by the other, the tournament director or the designated representative may accept or reject the request. It is suggested that the match be observed before determining what, if any, action is to be taken. In addition, two line judges and a scorekeeper may also be designated to assist the referee in officiating the match.

B.4 RULES BRIEFING
Before all tournaments, all officials and players shall be briefed on rules as well as local court hinders, regulations, and modifications the tournament director wishes to impose. The briefing should be reduced to writing. The current USRA rules will apply and be made available. Any modifications the tournament director wishes to impose must be stated on the entry form and be available to all players at registration.

B.5 REFEREES
(a) Pre-Match Duties. Before each match begins, it shall be the duty of the referee to:

1. Check on adequacy of preparation of court with respect to cleanliness, lighting and temperature.

2. Check on availability and suitability of materials to include balls, towels, scorecards, pencils and timepiece necessary for the match.

3. Check the readiness and qualifications of the line judges and scorekeeper. Review appeal procedures and instruct them of their duties, rules and local regulations.

4. Go onto the court to make introductions; brief the players on court hinders (both designated and undesignated); identify any out-of-play areas [see rule 2.1(a)]; discuss local regulations and rule modifications for this tournament; and explain often mis-interpreted rules.

5. Inspect players' equipment; identify the line judges; verify selection of a primary and alternate ball.

6. Toss coin and offer the winner the choice of serving or receiving.

(b) Decisions. During the match, the referee shall make all decisions with regard to the rules. Where line judges are used, the referee shall announce all final judgments. If both players in singles and three out of four in a doubles match disagree with a call made by the referee, the referee is overruled, with the exception of technical fouls and forfeitures.

(c) Protests. Any decision not involving the judgment of the referee will, on protest, be accorded due process as set forth in the constitution of the USRA. For the purposes of rendering a prompt decision regarding protests filed during the course of an ongoing tournament, the stages of due process will be: first to the tournament desk, then to the tournament director, and finally to the tournament rules committee. In those instances when time permits, the protest may be elevated to the state association or, when appropriate, to the national level as called for in the USRA constitution.

(d) Forfeitures. A match may be forfeited by the referee when:

1. Any player refuses to abide by the referee's decision or engages in unsportsmanlike conduct.

2. Any player or team who fails to report to play 10 minutes after the match has been scheduled to play. (The tournament director may permit a longer delay if circumstances warrant such a decision.)

3. A game will be forfeited by the referee for using an illegal racquet as specified in Rule 2.4(e).

(e) Defaults. A player or team may be forfeited by the tournament director or official for failure to comply with the tournament or host facility's rules while on the premises between matches, or for abuse of hospitality, locker room, or other rules and procedures.

(f) Spectators. The referee shall have jurisdiction over the spectators, as well as the players, while the match is in progress.

(g) Other Rulings. The referee may rule on all matters not covered in the USRA Official Rules. However, the referee's ruling is subject to protest as described in B.5 (c).

B.6 LINE JUDGES
(a) When Utilized. Two line judges should be used for semifinal and final matches, when requested by a player or team, or when the referee or tournament director so desires. However, the use of line judges is subject to availability and the discretion of the tournament director.

(b) Replacing Line Judges. If any player objects to a person serving as a line judge before the match begins, all reasonable effort shall be made to find a replacement acceptable to the officials and players. If a player objects after the match begins, any replacement shall be at the discretion of the referee and/or tournament director.

(c) Position of Line Judges. The players and referee shall designate the court location of the line judges. The tournament director shall settle any dispute.

(d) Duties and Responsibilities. Line judges are designated to help decide appeals. In the event of an appeal, and after a very brief explanation of the appeal by the referee, the line judges must indicate their opinion of the referee's call.

(e) Signals. Line judges should extend their arm and signal as follows: (i) thumb up to show agreement with the referee's call, (ii) thumb down to show disagreement, and (iii) hand open with palm facing down to indicate "no opinion" or that the play in question wasn't seen.

(f) Manner of Response. Line judges should be careful not to signal until the referee announces the appeal and asks for a ruling. In responding to the referee's request, line judges should not look at each other, but indicate their opinions simultaneously in clear view of the players and referee. If at any time a line judge is unsure of which call is being appealed or what the referee's call was, the line judge should ask the referee to repeat the call and the appeal.

(g) Result of Response. The referee's call stands if at least one line judge agrees with the referee or if neither line judge has an opinion. If both line judges disagree with the referee, the referee must reverse the call. If one line judge disagrees with the referee and the other signals no opinion, the rally is replayed. Any replays, with the exception of appeals on the second serve itself, will result in resumption of play at first serve.

B.7 APPEALS

(a) Appealable Calls and Non-Calls. In any match using line judges, a player may appeal any call or non-call by the referee, except for a technical foul or forfeiture.

(b) How to Appeal. A verbal appeal by a player must be made directly to the referee immediately after the rally has ended. A player who believes there is an infraction to appeal, should bring it to the attention of the referee and line judges by raising the non-racquet hand at the time the perceived infraction occurs. The player is obligated to continue to play until the rally has ended or the referee stops play. The referee will recognize a player's appeal only if it is made before that player leaves the court for any reason including timeouts and game-ending rallies or, if that player doesn't leave the court, before the next serve begins.

(c) Loss of Appeal. A player or team forfeits its right of appeal for that rally if the appeal is made directly to the line judges or, if the appeal is made after an excessive demonstration or complaint.

(d) Limit on Appeals. A player or team can make three appeals per game. However, if either line judge disagrees (thumb down) with the referee's call, that appeal will not count against the three-appeal limit. In addition, a potential game-ending rally may be appealed without charge against the limit—even if the three-appeal limit has been reached.

B.8 OUTCOME OF APPEALS

Everything except technical fouls and forfeitures can be appealed. The following outcomes cover several of the most common types of appeal, but not all possible appeals could be addressed. Therefore, referee's discretion and common sense should govern the outcomes of those appeals that are not covered herein:

(a) Skip Ball. If the referee makes a call of "skip ball," and the call is reversed, the referee then must decide if the shot in question could have been returned had play continued. If, in the opinion of the referee, the shot could have been returned, the rally shall be replayed. However, if the shot was irretrievable, the side that hit the shot in question is declared the winner of the rally. If the referee makes no call on a shot (thereby indicating that the shot did not skip), an appeal may be made that the shot skipped. If the "no call" is reversed, the side that hit the shot in question loses the rally.

(b) Fault Serve. If the referee makes a call of fault serve and the call is reversed, the serve is replayed - unless the referee considered the serve to have been irretrievable,

in which case a point is awarded to the server. If an appeal is made because the referee makes no call on a serve (thereby indicating that the serve was good) and the "no call" is reversed, the result will be a fault serve.

(c) Out Serve. If the referee calls an "out serve", and the call is reversed, the serve will be replayed, unless the serve was obviously a fault too, in which case the call becomes fault serve. However, if the call is reversed and the serve was considered an ace, a point will be awarded. Also, if the referee makes no call on a serve—thereby indicating that the serve was good—but the "no call" is reversed, it results in an immediate loss of serve.

(d) Double Bounce Pickup. If the referee makes a call of two bounces, and the call is reversed, the rally is replayed, except if the player against whom the call was made hit a shot that could not have been retrieved, then that player wins the rally. (Before awarding a rally in this situation, the referee must be certain that the shot would not have been retrieved even if play had not been halted.) If an appeal is made because the referee makes no call thereby indicating that the get was not two bounces, and the "no call" is reversed, the player who made the two bounce pickup is declared the loser of the rally.

(e) Receiving Line Violation (Encroachment). If the referee makes a call of encroachment, but the call is overturned, the serve shall be replayed unless the return was deemed irretrievable in which case a sideout (or possibly a handout in doubles) should be called. When an appeal is made because the referee made no call, and the appeal is successful, the server is awarded a point.

(f) Court Hinder. If the referee makes a call of court hinder during a rally or return of serve, the rally is replayed. If the referee makes no call and a player feels that a court hinder occurred, that player may appeal. If the appeal is successful, the rally will be replayed. If a court hinder occurs on a second serve, play resumes at second serve.

B.9 RULE INTERPRETATIONS

If a player feels the referee has interpreted the rules incorrectly, the player may require the referee or tournament director to cite the applicable rule in the rulebook. Having discovered a misapplication or misinterpretation, the official must correct the error by replaying the rally, awarding the point, calling sideout, or taking other corrective measures.

C — ELIGIBILITY AND NATIONAL EVENTS

C.1 ELIGIBILITY

To be eligible to compete in any USRA sanctioned event, a player may not have earned in excess of $50,000 in cumulative, total prize monies per season [as of August 1, annually], as a direct result of competing in any professional tournament(s) so deemed by the USRA Board of Directors.

(a) Merchandise or travel expenses shall not be considered prize money, nor will their acceptance affect a player's eligibility.

(b) Any USRA member, regardless of eligibility, may compete in any division that offers prize money or merchandise at a USRA sanctioned tournament.

C.2 RE-ESTABLISHING ELIGIBILITY

A player may re-establish their eligibility to compete in any USRA sanctioned event by tendering a request in writing to the Executive Director of the USRA or a designated representative, citing professional season-end earnings [as of August 1] below the $50,000 level. Once earnings are verified, eligibility may be re-established, effective immediately.

C.3 WAIVER & RELEASE

Athletic Waiver and Release of Liability: In consideration of being allowed to participate in any United States Racquetball Association athletics/sports programs, and related events and activities, all member signators:

1. Agree that prior to participating, they will inspect the facilities and equipment to be used, and if they believe anything is unsafe, they will immediately advise their coach, supervisor, or USRA personnel of such condition(s) and refuse to participate.

2. Acknowledge and fully understand that each participant will be engaging in activities that involve risk of serious injury, including permanent disability and death, and severe social and economic losses which might result not only from their own actions, inactions of negligence but the actions, inactions or negligence of others, the rules of play, or the condition of the premises or of any equipment used. Further, that there may be other risks not known to us or not reasonably foreseeable at this time.

3. Assume all the foregoing risks and accept personal responsibility for the damages following such injury, permanent disability or death.

4. Release, waive, discharge and covenant not to sue the United States Racquetball Association, its affiliated clubs, regional sports organizations, their respective adminis-trators, directors, agents, coaches, and other employees of the organization, other participants, sponsoring agencies, sponsors, advertisers, and, if applicable, owners and lessees of premises used to conduct the event, all of which are hereinafter referred to as "releasees" from any and all liability to the signator on the opposite side of this form, his or her heirs and next of kin for any and all claims, demands, losses or damages on account of injury including death or damage to property, caused or alleged to be caused in whole or in part by the negligence of the release of otherwise.

C.4 RECOGNIZED DIVISIONS

Title opportunities at national championships will be selected from the division lists that follow. Combined "Age + Skill" divisions may also be offered to provide additional competitive opportunities for non-open entrants.

For ranking consistency, state organizations and tournament hosts should select from these recognized divisions when establishing competition in all sanctioned events.

(a) Open Division. Any eligible player, as defined in C.1.

(b) Adult Age Divisions. Eligibility is determined by the player's age on the first day of the tournament. Divisions are:
24 & under - Varsity
25+ - Junior Veterans
30+ - Veterans
35+ - Seniors
40+ - Veteran Seniors
45+ - Masters
50+ - Veteran Masters
55+ - Golden Masters
60+ - Veteran Golden Masters
65+ - Senior Golden Masters
70+ - Advanced Golden Masters
75+ - Super Golden Masters
80+ - Grand Masters
85+ - Super Grand Masters

(c) Junior Age Divisions. Player eligibility is determined by the player's age on January 1st of the current calendar year. Divisions are:
18 & Under
16 & Under
14 & Under
12 & Under
10 & Under
8 & Under (regular rules)
8 & Under (multi-bounce rules)
6 & Under (regular rules)
6 & Under (multi-bounce rules)

(d) Skill Divisions. Player eligibility (in "lettered" divisions) is determined by AmPRO skill certification, or verification by a state association official, at the entered level.

Elite

A

B

C

D

Novice

(e) Age + Skill Divisions. Player eligibility is determined by the player's age on the first day of the tournament, plus AmPRO skill level certification, or verification by a state association official, at the entered level. Such combinations may be offered as additional competition to players who do not fall into the "open" or designated skill levels of play. For example: 24- A/B; 35+ C/D; 40+ A/B; 65+ A/B, etc.

C.5 COMPETITION BY GENDER

Men and women may compete only in events and divisions for their respective gender during regional and national tournaments. If there is not sufficient number of players to warrant play in a specific division, the tournament director may place the entrants in a comparably competitive division. Note: For the purpose of encouraging the development of women's racquetball, the governing bodies of numerous states permit women to play in men's divisions when a comparable skill level is not available in the women's divisions.

C.6 USRA REGIONAL CHAMPIONSHIPS

Eligibility: Only U.S. citizens may compete in any division of play that serves as a qualifier for an event that offers appointment to a U.S. National Team (adult or junior). All other divisions are open to U.S. citizens and residents.

(a) Regional tournaments will be conducted at various metropolitan sites designated annually by the USRA and players may compete at any site they choose.

(b) A person may compete in any number of adult regional tournaments, but may not enter a championship division (as listed in C.4) after having won that division at a previous adult regional tournament that same year.

(c) A person cannot participate in more than two championship events at a regional tournament.

(d) Any awards or remuneration to a USRA National Championship will be posted on the entry blank.

C.7 U.S. NATIONAL CHAMPIONSHIPS

Eligibility: Only U.S. citizens may compete in any division of play that serves as a qualifier for appointment

to a U.S. National Team (adult or junior). All other divisions are open to U.S. citizens and residents.

C.8 EVENTS & QUALIFIERS
(a) U.S. NATIONAL SINGLES AND DOUBLES CHAMPIONSHIPS

The U.S. National Singles and Doubles Tournaments are separate tournaments and are played on different dates. National Singles are traditionally held in May; National Doubles in October.

Competition in an Adult Regional singles tournament (or recognized qualifying event) is required to qualify for the National Singles Championship.

Recognized qualifying events are: WSMA Championships (January); NMRA Singles Championships (February); Intercollegiate Championships (April); U.S. Military Championships.

Exemptions: Alaska/Hawaii residents; active duty overseas military.

(b) U.S. NATIONAL JUNIOR OLYMPIC CHAMPI-ONSHIPS
It will be conducted on a different date than all other National Championships. Traditionally held in June.

Competition in a Level Three State Singles tournament (or recognized qualifying event) is required to qualify for the Junior Olympic Championship.

Recognized qualifying events are: formal junior qualifier; National High School Championships (March).

(c) U.S. NATIONAL HIGH SCHOOL CHAMPIONSHIPS
It will be conducted on a different date than all other National Championships. Traditionally held in March.

(d) U.S. NATIONAL INTERCOLLEGIATE CHAMPIONSHIPS
It will be conducted on a different date than all other National Championships. Traditionally held in April.

(e) U.S. OPEN RACQUETBALL CHAMPIONSHIPS
It will be conducted on a different date than all other National Championships, and include both pro and USRA divisions. Traditionally held in November.

D — PROCEDURES

D.1 RULE CHANGE PROCEDURES
To ensure the orderly growth of racquetball, the USRA has established specific procedures that are followed before a major change is made to the rules of the game.

NOTE: Changes to rules and regulations in Sections 1 through 10 must adhere to published rule change procedures. Remaining sections may be altered by vote of the USRA Board of Directors*.

(a) Rule change proposals must be submitted in writing to the USRA National Office by June 1st. NOTE: The Board of Directors has imposed a moratorium on rule changes that establishes the next deadline for submission of rule change proposals as June 1, 2002, which would set the earliest possible effective date as September 1, 2003. [See following timeline for procedural details.]

(b) The USRA Board of Directors will review all proposals at its October board meeting and determine which will be considered.

(c) Selected proposals will appear in RACQUETBALL Magazine — the official USRA publication — as soon as possible after the October meeting for comment by the general membership.

(d) After reviewing membership input and the recommendations of the National Rules Committee and National Rules Commissioner, the proposals are discussed and voted upon at the annual Board of Directors meeting in May.

(e) Changes approved in May become effective on September 1st. Exception: changes in racquet specifications become effective two years later on September 1st.

(f) Proposed rules that are considered for adoption in one year, but are not approved by the Board of Directors in May of that year, will not be considered for adoption the following year.

* The following "policies & procedures" segments are subject to stated rule change procedures outlined in D.1:
A.6 Round Robin Scoring
A.8 Tournament Conduct
B.5 (d-g) Forfeitures, Defaults ...
B.6 Line Judges
B.7 Appeals
B.8 Outcome of Appeals

D.2 NATIONAL RULES COMMITTEE

Rich Clay, National Rules Commissioner
3401 North Kedzie
Chicago, IL 60618
773/539-1114 (Office)
847/918-7407 (Home)

Michael Arnolt
Suite 307
3833 North Meridian Street
Indianapolis, IN 46208
317/926-2766 (Office)
317/259-1359 (Home)

Dan Davis
5304 Hollister Street
Houston, TX 77040
713/409-3838 (Home)
713/895-8588 (Office)

Otto Dietrich
4244 Russet Court
Lilburn, GA 30047
770/972-2303 (Home)

Jim Easterling
321 Village
Lansing, MI 48911
517/887-0459 (Home)
517/373-2399 (Office)

Lorraine Galloway
175-20 Wexford Terrace #7-S
Jamaica Estates, NY 11432
718/739-4629 (Home)

Jim Gillhouse
2120 East Willamette Avenue
Colorado Springs, CO 80909
719/471-0799 (Home)
719/651-9600 (Office)

Mary Lyons
940 Penman Road
Neptune Beach, FL 32266
904/270-2224 (Office)

Eric Muller
445 Fifth Avenue, Apt. 32C
New York, NY 10016
212-683-1610 (Home)

Annie Muniz
812 Woodstock
Bellaire, TX 77401
713/659-3554 (Office)
713/432-0881 (Home)

RULEBOOK INDEX